You GET ONE SHOT

AT LIFE

AIM FOR SUCCESS

Secrets of
Living a Meaningful Life

Aaron Lumpkin

Cover and Interior Design: www.book-cover-design.com

PUBLISHED BY
Winning Publications
P. O. Box 60443
Nashville, TN 37206-0443
FAX: 615 258 3728
e-mail: winningpublish@aol.com

Publisher's Cataloging-in-Publication Data

Lumpkin, Aaron.
You get one shot at life—aim for success:
secrets of living a meaningful life / Aaron Lumpkin.
p. cm.
Includes bibliographical references and index.
LCCN 2005900905
ISBN 0-9711605-2-X
1. Success 2. Self-realization. 3. Conduct of Life I. Title
BF637.S8L.86 2005
158.1
QB105-600011

Printed In the United States of America

You GET ONE SHOT
AT LIFE
AIM FOR SUCCESS

*Secrets of
Living a Meaningful Life*

Aaron Lumpkin

Winning Publications

Contents

Introduction

Sandy Walters had it all. She was God's gift to the world. She was chosen Homecoming Queen and Cheerleading Captain. She had been the Student Council's Vice-President in the 11th grade and President in the 12th grade; Class Favorite in the 10th and 11th grades, and a member of the Beta Club for four years. Her life seemed almost perfect. She was smart, beautiful, and popular.

I was reading about Ms. Walters while waiting to speak to the inmates at a women's prison. When I entered the dull, dreary room where the women were kept, I noticed that some of the ladies were so unkempt that they didn't seem to care how they looked. All the women were wearing the same prison attire: red shirts and pants that didn't fit. Some of the ladies were wearing signs around their necks with various messages on them such as, "I must listen better," or "I talk too much." These were grown women. Their faces had defeated looks and many of the ladies did not seem to care about anything. Their spirits were broken because they had suffered a lot of discouragement.

The contrast between the Homecoming Queen and inmates was striking. The Homecoming Queen probably woke up eager to begin her day while many of the women in the prison woke up dreading their day—and some would rather be dead.

The contrast struck me so dramatically that I felt driven to understand why some people seem to have everything and for others mere existence is hell. I became resolved to encourage people who feel they are only average to reach for the stars, and from that moment on, I have devoted a large part of my life to that cause. I have triumphed over adversity in my own life, and because of my success, I believe that everyone has what it takes to live meaningful lives.

We get one shot at life. If our lives lack meaning, happiness and purpose, we need to consider how not to throw our lives away through apathy, indifference, self-pity and hopelessness. We can't allow other people's opinions, our learned behaviors, self-doubts, our poor self-images, our misfortunes, and our unwise choices to keep us from living rich, meaningful and exciting lives. **We have the right to be happy.**

There are two main reasons why many of us do not live more colorful, energetic, enthusiastic, compelling, and inspiring lives. First, many of us have not made a diligent effort to overcome the negative feelings that we have developed over the years. Some of us have decided that we are not smart enough, not lucky enough, not deserving of a better existence, so we resign ourselves to living mediocre lives.

The second reason is that we have allowed *others* to determine whether or not we are happy. Society says we must be good-looking, educated, accomplished, wealthy, and clever to have true value in this world. And who is making all these rules? People—imperfect people who in many cases operate largely out of self interest, people who don't know what they really want, people who talk a lot but say little, people who play psychological games.

It's time to see life for what is really is. All the rewards in life do not go to the lucky, the strong, the wealthy, the attractive, or the popular. The true rewards go to those who are able to see life for what it really is—**a fascinating and complex experience.**

Right now would be a great time to reflect on our lives and ask ourselves some serious questions. Have we resolved to live our lives the way we currently are? Is there anything that can be improved? Are we running on automatic and simply responding to stimulus? Are we **waiting** on something to motivate us to live more exciting lives?

This book is written for people who are not perfect and know that they are not perfect. The book is for people who do not have their lives totally together. Many people act as if they have no problems, trying to convince other people that they have it all together. But, even if they are not honest enough right now to recognize their problems, eventually they will have to. Life itself will make them honest.

Life is a struggle for all of us. I have made mistakes and I continue to mistakes. The Bible says all of us are imperfect. So why can't we share our humanity in a spirit of helping and encouraging one another? Whether we are wrestling with lust, pride, envy, selfishness, lack of confidence, poor self-concept, or the loss of a loved one, life can be a daily challenge—and we need to realize this fact.

It doesn't do anyone any good to go through life pretending that everything is ok when everything is not ok.

All of us are imperfect.

CHAPTER ONE

Making Our Lives Count

—LIVING LIVES THAT MATTER—

*W*hy is life such a challenge? Why does life seem more wearisome for some people than it is for others? Why do some people seem to have all the fun and all the luck? Why are so many people unable to find real meaning and happiness in life?

Is it possible for us to find more excitement, adventure, romance, and experience more of the feelings that make us **feel alive**? Is there some central truth that will help us live richer, more rewarding lives? Is there anything we can do to live more dynamic lives **right now**? The answer to these questions is a resounding yes! There are actions we can take that will help us live successful lives.

We're going to take a journey together through the pages of this book. We're going to see that all of us have the potential to live meaningful lives.

Maybe life makes no sense to you. Possibly you just need to be motivated. Perhaps you have low self-esteem and a poor self-image. Maybe you are struggling with alcohol or drugs. It could be that you just need a little guidance and direction to get your life on track. You may be confused and scared, troubled by life in general. Maybe you just need something or someone to jumpstart your life. Whatever the case, if you are interested in turning your life around, **it is possible.**

We are going to take an honest look at ourselves and see what we can do to get our lives on track because we only get **one chance at life.** We do not get to start over. Each moment of life is precious, whether we realize it or not. People are responding to us **right now** based on the way we are acting. That's right. You and I are actually determining how the world treats us **right now.** If we are not satisfied, then we need to focus on transforming ourselves.

In this book, we will be considering some exciting concepts. We will see why the world is such a challenging place. We will look at some of the greatest emotional dangers that we will face and how to avoid them. We will learn how to wake ourselves up if we are taking life for granted.

We will also look at how we can make sense of ourselves, the world in general, and how to improve our relationships. We will discuss how to become more confident and courageous so that we can live more fulfilling lives. We will consider how to put our lives back together if we have made some unwise choices. We will learn how to make a plan that that will start us down a new road of adventure.

I'm on your side. I want you to win at the game of life. If you are really interested in getting your life together, put everything you can into this book. Give it your best shot. When you see how stimulating life can be, you will begin to strive even harder. I guarantee you that I will not waste your time. I promise that you can have more good times, more excitement, and more adventure. Life is not an experience to dread everyday, but a fascinating adventure! That's **great** news!

Today is a new day of opportunity. There is just no telling what you could become. You have no idea the excitement awaiting you. Give life your best shot. I'm going to help you see the real *you* that is trying to get out!

Start Making The Most
Of Your Life Today

My goal is for you to decide today that you are going to start taking action. Life does not wait for us. Universities begin classes at definite times. The four seasons are on a set schedule. There are only certain seasons in which various sports can be played.

We are getting a little older every day. We need to be careful not to have a "one of these days I am going to change my life" attitude.

You need someone to encourage you. You need someone to cheer you on. I will be your coach. As far as your life is concerned, **today is your day**.

There are many ways to approach transforming our lives and developing a more optimistic attitude. But, if you are like me, you want to feel better now. So I want to ask you to decide in your **heart** right now that you are not going to **throw away your one shot at life**. Just say to yourself right now, "I am not going to throw away my life." This decision is actually a good start.

Who Are You And What
Do You Want Out Of Life?

Some of us are very attractive; some of us are typical

looking. Some of us are extremely athletic or musically talented; others are not. Some of us are very clever and humorous and some of us are a little boring. Some of us feel like the world belongs to us and some of us feel almost too ashamed to exist.

What do you really want out of life? Do you want to be more attractive? Do you want to help people or change the world? Do you want to find peace of mind? What do you really want?

No matter who we are, all of us are going through the human experience together. None of us asked to be here. We just awakened one day and noticed that we were in this thing called life. As we grew, we noticed there were nice people, jerks, large people, mean people, stuck-up girls and guys, bullies, sickness, poverty, death, pain, drugs, and violence. We noticed that in many cases, people who were more attractive than others often seemed to be more popular. We noticed that people who had money seemed to have more and seemed to feel that they were better than everyone else. We noticed that our shortcomings, whether mental or physical, worked against us. People put us down and made us feel inferior while others used their assets to their advantage.

Throughout my life, I have noticed that the rewards of life do not go to any certain group of people, even the lucky and the strong. The true rewards such as peace of mind and joy go to those who search for knowledge and the *true* meaning of life.

To develop a deeper sense of the meaning, we should center our attention on seeking wisdom and understanding. If we are not careful, we will throw away our lives by allowing the world and its standards to determine how we feel about ourselves. **The real truth is that all of us have the potential to live meaningful and rewarding lives.** This is not just something nice to say to make you feel good. The fact is that all of us are incredible people, but if we do not realize this fact, we may miss the true excitement that life has to offer.

I'm convinced that all of us are here for a reason. All of us have a purpose for existing. But if we cannot believe that we have a purpose, we may drift through life like a raft lost on the ocean.

I want to help you see your **true value** as a human being so that you can begin living the meaningful and rewarding life you were meant to live. Start your new life today by resolving that you have had enough of feeling less than great.

Your life can be a fascinating adventure. Begin your quest by improving your aim at a better life.

Reaching For
A Higher Level Of Serenity

Two main purposes of this book are to encourage us to capitalize on our strengths and to expand our way of looking at ourselves. All of us have our own particular challenges to face: loneliness, depression, poor self-concept, anger, revenge, jealousy, envy, feelings of hopelessness, lack of meaning, sickness, lack of confidence, drug/alcohol problems, feelings of insecurity, lust, or fear. Now is the time to reach for the next level in life, rather than hanging on to these negative feelings.

We are going to unlock some of the mysteries of life. As you go through this book, focus on the following principles:

1. You are not only the physical person you were born to be, but you are also the person you have the potential to be.

2. Fate and destiny favor the brave and courageous.

3. The only way we will ever be great is not through what we do with our bodies, but what we do with our minds.

4. People who consider life boring and uninspiring have not had anyone teach them how to dream.

5. People who live mediocre lives are often hypnotized by their environment by things such as the media, television, and ideals that no one can truly attain.

6. It is not so much what we know as it is knowing that life is a great mystery.

7. Most of us live out of habitual feelings, so we tend to experience the same reality everyday, over and over. We become stuck in our emotions because we have not learned how to raise our awareness.

8. We are not in the condition we are in by chance or accident. Our thoughts, aims, and actions have put us where we are.

9. All of us are ruled by our habits. To be successful, we have to develop better habits.

10. Either we develop better habits, or our habits control us.

My goal is to help you reach the next level in your life. I am going to offer you help instead of blame, support instead of judgment, and information rather than condemnation. My desire is to help you develop a new perspective on your life, so that you may find for yourself some of the meaning and happiness that you are searching for.

There is hope. I know it is possible to turn our lives around because I have seen it happen in my own life. My main goal here is to plant a seed of hope that your life can change, too.

First, we will consider **seven important principles for success.** I will be elaborating on these basic principles throughout the book.

Seven Basic Concepts Of Success

1. When we respond or react to other people negatively, we often do not realize what kind of experience they are having. They may be angry, frustrated, or confused. If other people treat us badly and we let the experience make us feel bad, we are being unfair to ourselves by assuming that the negative feelings of other people are aimed at us. In most cases, this is the farthest thing from the truth.

2. Few situations are going to happen in life that we don't cause to happen. Life is not about luck. Whatever we want in life, we must go after. When we realize that nothing is going to fall into our laps, we can really begin taking responsibility for our own happiness.

3. We have more personal power than we realize. All of us have the potential to stand up for ourselves. If we believe that we do not have personal power, we are going to constantly hold ourselves back.

4. We must realize our true value as humans. Even though we may not be as attractive, wealthy, or smart as others, we still have value and purpose. If we do not realize how precious we are, the world will run over us.

5. It is important for us to spend some time trying to determine why we act the way we do. All of us have character defects and shortcomings. If we are not aware of our imperfections, we will repeat our negative patterns without even realizing it.

6. Realize that life is not fair. If we received the short straw in one area or another, we need to compensate for our shortcomings rather than spend our lives being depressed.

7. Try to see life as it is, not as we wish it were or the way we think it should be. Often we live in our own little world and not in reality. If we are not able to see past our own experience, we are destined to live out our lives in our own little bubble, perhaps missing great opportunities for happiness.

These seven concepts will help you to start thinking about your life differently. Now, let's also consider *why* we don't strive harder to live more exciting lives.

The Greatest Obstacle Keeping Us From Living A Meaningful Life

The greatest obstacle to making positive changes in our lives is lack of **drive**. There is a lot of information available to help us change our lives, but the information is of no use if we just don't feel like changing. **Many of us hold ourselves back because we just can't seem to lift ourselves out of our**

present frame of mind. It's like trying to lose weight. Most of us would like to lose weight and look better, so why do so many of us not even try? **We just don't want to. It's too much trouble.** We deceive ourselves into thinking that life is for the attractive, the lucky, and the strong. We say, "Why should I deprive myself when I will probably fail anyway? I am what I am and nothing can change that."

I have picked up lots of books similar to this one and read 30 or 40 pages, became bored, and then just put them away in my house somewhere. Some of the books seem to ask too much of me and want me to give more than I am able to give. Often the information is glorified, unrealistic, and syrupy.

My main goal is to help you develop the *desire* to live a more fulfilling life. I am a fairly average person. Sometimes life is very challenging for me. Sometimes I get depressed. Sometimes, I wish I were younger, wealthier, and better looking. Sometimes, I absolutely love life. The important fact is that I have come a long way from where I was in the past. I lived most of my life with poor self-esteem, a negative self-concept, and a cynical attitude.

If this book helps at least one person on the planet to see him or herself in a better way, then it would have been worth it. In a relatively short few years, I will no longer be here, but the principles and ideas discussed here will remain the same today or a thousand years from now.

A Wake Up Call

The information in this book is a wake up call. We never really know what kind of person or situation is going to affect us. Recently, I was profoundly encouraged by two twelve-year-old girls. One girl was blind. The other girl had only one arm, because her other arm had been bitten off by a shark while she was floating on her surfboard.

I saw the blind girl, Brittney Luna, singing in front of a small group of people. She was an excellent singer, but what really impressed me about her was how comfortable she was with herself. She was very relaxed with the audience, and she seemed not overly concerned about what the crowd thought of her if she forgot some lyrics. She was not egotistical, shy, or overbearing. She did not "put on airs," and she did not act like she had anything to prove. I don't think I have ever seen a human be so natural. Her behavior seemed to say, "This is life, people. Let's enjoy it while we can."

After she finished singing, I told her how much her performance meant to me. After I told her, the first thing she said to me was, "I need a hug!" She had never met me before, but she seemed to have a natural love for life and people. I do not often see this kind of love for life. I believe this lovely young lady is the kind of person who is going to encourage and bring meaning into the lives of thousands of people, even though she can't see. **To me, she can see much better than the rest of us.**

The other young lady, Bethany Hamilton, had met with misfortune while floating on her surfboard. Her arm was dangling in the water and a large shark came along and bit it off up to the shoulder. It was bad enough that she lost her arm, but the situation was compounded by the fact that she was an extremely promising surfer.

When Bethany was interviewed by the media, she asserted that she had to keep a good attitude so that her family and friends would not be sad. She had to keep herself upbeat and keep on going so she could accomplish her goals. To top it off, she could not wait to get back to surfing! **She was so full of love and courage.** (Check out her web site! www.bethany-hamilton.com).

Both of these girls humbled me. Without realizing it, they helped me to explain the central idea in this book. Both of these girls have severe limitations, yet through their positive attitudes they bring more meaning into their lives and the lives of others than many of us who have no true limitations. **Many of us never truly learn to live, to realize what is important in life, or to truly encourage others.** It's not so much that we are bad people, it's just that we are driven by our learned behaviors, our habits, and our environments.

It takes a lot of honesty to see ourselves as we really are. I have seen and met many different kinds of people in my life: politicians, great speakers, movie stars, business executives, scientists, and physicians. But few have compelled me to want to live a more meaningful life than those two twelve-year-old girls. My hope is that by mentioning them in this book, thousands of other people will also be encouraged and inspired to live richer and more rewarding lives now, rather than letting limitations—real or imagined—determine our level of happiness forever.

Today is a new day for us. **We are still here; we still have a chance. Resolve to begin a new life today. Life is amazing! Don't miss out on it!**

QUESTIONS TO PONDER

- Are you sincerely warm and friendly with other people? Do you add joy to their lives?

- How would your life be different if you lost a limb or became blind?

- Do you think that it is possible that many people are "blind" to what is really important in life?

- What would it take for you to develop the **desire** to live a rewarding, fulfilling life?

CHAPTER TWO

Why is Life Such a Challenge?

*I*t's a typical Tuesday morning as I drive into work. A lot of people are obviously late because they are speeding around haphazardly. Some of the women walking into the office buildings appear to have quickly thrown their clothes together and some of the men must not have made time to shave. As I arrive at work, I see the same people arriving who have worked at the same place for years. Everyday is the same. Some just show up and wait for retirement.

The daily news sounds the same. The events of the world seem far away and too big to think about.

Many people seem to be just going through the motions. Friends meet at the water coolers to discuss their personal problems. Other groups of people are discussing sports or whatever comes to mind. Most of them seem lost in their own little world. Their faces seem to say, "I do not know how to enjoy life. I must fulfill my obligations and somehow get through the day."

I'm in another one of my thinking moods. Does my life matter? Am I making any kind of difference in the world? I can see my life slowly drifting away. I am 52 at this moment. Sometimes, I wish I were 30. I know that I am not going to live forever, perhaps not even much longer. How can I live in such a way now to make sure my life has real meaning for myself and others?

It's so easy to let the days seem humdrum. Some days seem very good and other days seem not so good. I know that on the good days, life is an exciting, marvelous miracle, but what about the days that don't feel exciting? Don't they take up as much time as the good days?

Sometimes, I have loved life. Other times, I have not cared much for it. My life peaked when I met the girl who was to become my wife, when my son was born, and when I gave my first public speech. I went down into a dark valley when I lost both my parents within two years, when my 22-year old brother was killed in a hideous wreck, when my first child died at birth, and when I fought a battle with alcohol.

Sometimes, as I have walked through life, I have felt as though I were holding hands with God. At other times, I have felt that God could care less about me.

I have dealt with people who thought they were the only people in the universe and other people who thought they were scum.

I have learned that the best way to approach life is with honesty. Like all other people, I have had many up and down experiences. I am not going to sugarcoat life in this book.

The purpose of this book is to help you develop a better understanding of life so that you will have a chance to really enjoy it. We are going to begin by considering why things are the way they are. In other words, why is life so hard? Why isn't life easier?

Many people are confused by life at this point in history. Wars, famine, and disease ravish the planet. We are killing our environments, and more people are living in poverty than ever before.

Many people are simply drifting along with the everyday flow of life. They have some fun and exciting experiences, but when the fun is over, they still feel empty. Their lives seem to lack true meaning. Some people can't stand reality so they drink too much or resort to drugs or both. Some people find temporary meaning only in pleasurable feelings. Still others find a false sense of contentment through status, money, looks, power and various other worldly pursuits or attributes.

The bottom line is that even these people are often not truly happy and content. Life does not make sense to a lot of people. We are going to learn how to make sense of life because our time here is shorter than we realize and we do not want to throw it away chasing meaningless pursuits.

The First Reason
Life Is Such A Challenge

The beginning of learning how to live more meaningful lives is realizing why life is such a challenge. In other words, why does life seem so difficult sometimes? Why is life such a struggle? Well, the first reason life is so challenging is because **people are the way they are**. Why is this fact significant? People run the world--the physical world itself is just here. Think about it. People run schools, businesses, the government, hospitals, and churches. All relationships and interactions between people are governed by the attitudes and beliefs that people hold. **If people are biased, shallow, wrong, selfish, misguided, ignorant, or narrowly-focused, other people are going to suffer because of their beliefs and actions.**

People are not going to act any differently until they **change**. Understand this fact and you will be off to a good start toward understanding life. Don't waste a lot of energy wishing people would act differently. They won't act any differently until they decide to make some changes.

For life to be different, one or more of three situations has to happen: either other people change, or we change, or both.

People are basically "stuck" where they are. Until people raise their level of awareness, they will continue acting and responding in the same ways. So we should not be surprised when people keep acting the same ways over and over. The truth is: **They don't know any other way to act**.

Carefully consider what we are saying here. When two or more people gather together in a social group, the outcomes of their social interactions are predictable. The same social interactions play out over and over. For example, educated people tend to hang out with and gravitate towards other educated people. People with low self-esteem tend to hang out with other people who have low self-esteem. People who curse will hang out with other people who curse. Religious people tend to hang out with other religious people. Stuck-up people hang out with other stuck-up people. **People who have similar ideals and beliefs will hang out together, because most people need others to help convince them that their beliefs are correct**.

Do you see the point? People really are fairly predictable. There are patterns to the way people act, and this is one reason the world stays the way it is. All people have learned to behave a certain way. They will stay that way until they decide to change or until something causes them to change.

Even your family doctor validates the reality that we do have predictable patterns of behavior. When your doctor asks you about your family history, he knows that certain inherited characteristics and even lifestyles determine the kind of health you have. We inherit genes from our parents and we tend to develop their lifestyles. These inherited genes and lifestyles lead to **predictable outcomes**.

The reason we are considering people and their predictable behaviors is that we often allow other people's opinions of us to determine how we feel about ourselves. When we realize that other people are going to continually act in the same ways, we will begin to see that life will only get better for us when we make **some changes in our lives**.

It is very important to understand that if neither us nor other people make any changes, there is going to be human gridlock in our lives. When this occurs, we may choose to go through life wondering why life does not get better when the truth is we are involved in a massive "mind jam" where none of us are willing to change.

It is like two political parties who both believe that they hold the absolute truth. In the end, neither party accomplishes all they would like to because both parties are too blind to see that they both cannot be completely right.

Likewise, if our thoughts are holding us back because we are blind to the truth about ourselves, **we are destined to stay the way we are forever**.

Starting today, begin focusing on getting back into life. Many of us have gotten sidetracked by various circumstances, situations, and misguided thoughts. Some of us have lost our perspective on life and we don't have a lot of direction. Let's start from scratch and begin raising our level of awareness. **Let's at least do something. Life is out there waiting.**

Let's begin our new life by realizing that **life is happening inside our minds.** If we were to die tonight, all of the people, circumstances, events, and happenings that were in our minds would not even exist, at least as far as we are concerned.

In a way, all of us live in our own little world. Each new morning, we are on our own little "trip." Our minds are like cameras recording the events of our lives. The world is the stage. It is important for us to realize that everything that happens to us is going on inside our heads, because **only then can we begin to see that it is not the life outside our heads that is determining our happiness, but the way we perceive life in our minds.**

It should be apparent that if we are dissatisfied with our lives, we will probably need to make to **make some changes in the way we think about life.** At this point, we just want to become aware of how our minds interact with the world around us. We want to come to a better understanding of why things are the way they are. Remember, things are the way they are is because *people* are the way they are.

Let's take some examples to help us understand the ideas that we have discussed so far. We are going consider several people and how their minds shape the way they see life so far.

Janet

Janet is an average looking girl in high school. She is not the most popular nor the least popular girl in her school. Janet feels confused because she finds that other guys and girls are difficult to understand. The various students seem to be coming from a thousand directions.

Janet notices that the students exhibit the same behaviors over and over. The guys flirt with the cutest girls. The smartest students flaunt pretentious attitudes. The meanest students push the weaker students around. Each day is the same.

Janet yearns to live a more exciting and meaningful life but she feels trapped in her own lifestyle of mediocrity. She feels helpless and dependent on her environment. She believes that she does not have enough confidence to live the kind of life she dreams of. She desires to become an independent, authentic, and fulfilled human being—a winner.

Johnny

Johnny is bored with life. His main satisfaction comes from pleasurable feelings, but inside he feels that something is missing from his life. His soul is telling him that there has got to be more to life than simply having a good time. Johnny wants to accomplish something. He does not want to throw his life away chasing feelings that do not bring long-lasting satisfaction. He wants people to know that his life means something, and he wants to bring meaning into the lives of other people. He just does not know how.

Betty

Betty is wrestling with alcohol and drugs, especially pot and crack. Betty has always had a hard time understanding life. She got part of her low self-esteem from her parents. Betty feels rather lost in the world at times. With each day that passes, she sees herself as more of a rebel.

But she sees the insane busy lifestyles of other people and knows she doesn't want that, either. She sees many people who seem to be living shallow lives. Everyone is going their own way and doing their own thing. No one wants to be bothered. Betty sees very little hope for her future.

Cassie

Cassie is a very religious person. She finds much joy, satisfaction, and meaning in the spiritual pursuits of life. However, she sometimes feels disconnected from people who seem to be living more worldly lives. She sees the people around her becoming less spiritual and she sometimes feels like she could be missing something. She is aware of her own desires, and she just wants to be sure that she is living the best life that she can. She also realizes that the world is changing around her in drastic ways. Cassie wants to take some time to examine her life.

Regina

Regina is a person who has made some fairly serious mistakes in her life. Her biggest problem is that people will not let her off the hook. They constantly remind Regina of what a bad person she is. They constantly try to keep Regina in the box that they want her in. Regina tries to rise above her circumstances, but so far she has not had much success. Regina needs to reflect on her life and to realize that other people do not determine her value.

Caleb

Caleb is a person who sees himself in a negative way. He was a little rowdy in school and he came to view himself as a trouble maker. Therefore, in everything he does, he plays the role of a trouble maker. Caleb is unable to reach for the next level of life because he cannot see his real value as a person. He has labeled himself, and therefore he acts in accordance with what he believes is his true nature. Caleb is typical of many people, who believe that they are less than average and therefore they live their lives based on these imposed limitations. Caleb needs to do some soul-searching and find out who he truly is.

Maybe you can relate to one or more of these people. Perhaps you need to do some soul-searching so that you can get your life back on track. As we take this journey together, give it your all. **This is your life we are talking about.**

One Of The Great Secrets Of Life

Right here, I am going to tell you one of the secrets of life. The secret is **realizing that all of us bring something to life that others cannot bring**. All of us are extremely unique, but until we realize our own uniqueness, we are holding ourselves back in accomplishments and enjoyment.

You may be rich, poor, attractive, average, smart, athletic, or clumsy. **It is your imperfections that give you the drive for individual development.** Think about it. Disadvantages provide barriers that cause us to focus our energies in other areas. Your unique circumstances give you the experience and drive to do what you have been put here to do. If all of us were alike, we would all be doing the same thing!

All of us have a lot to offer in life. **(You are not the one exception!)** All of us are very special in our own right. For example, some people are well educated and they use their skills to make the world a better place. Some people are able to speak very eloquently and inspire others. Some of us are athletic, witty, friendly or compassionate. Some people focus on helping others through life. Some of us are artists, inventors, musicians, or scientists.

No one on Earth can bring to life what you bring. No one on earth has walked in your shoes. No one has had your particular experiences. You are truly an extraordinary individual.

If you want to win at life, focus on realizing your true value as a human.

You may have been put down or pushed around throughout your life. You may have been told that you are nothing and that you will never be anything. You may never have been told how precious you are. But I am telling you that you are somebody, and I encourage you to take your self-concept and self-esteem up another level this very day.

All of us need to feel a sense of self-worth. All of us need to feel loved, important, special, wanted, needed, and accepted. All of us need to feel that we have something special to offer the world.

If we want to change and live more rewarding lives, we should start by simply learning to believe that all of us have something truly distinctive to offer. Some of us have allowed other people to determine our value as humans. Some of us have spent our entire lives comparing ourselves to others. **It's time to get on track. The clock is ticking.**

Make the decision right now that you are going to stop holding yourself back. Decide right now to realize that you are just as special as everyone else. Start believing in your own worth. The way you see yourself is going to determine the kind of life you are going to live. **The way you see yourself will determine whether you win or lose, succeed or fail, and maybe even live or die. You get one chance at life.**

The Second Reason Why
Life Is So Challenging

So far, we have established the idea that the world is the way it is largely because people are the way they are. The world does not change until people change. We have discussed the idea that people are predictable--tomorrow morning, our family, friends, and other people are going to behave basically the same way they have always behaved. The same basic social situations are going to occur all over the world tomorrow. The people with the best self-esteem and the most confidence are going to receive more of the rewards of life. **Life is not going to surprise us tomorrow.**

But the second reason why life is so demanding is because **many of us do not do anything to change or improve ourselves**. We stay the same and so does our world. We touched on this idea in an earlier section, but now we are going to look more closely at our role in changing our lives.

Consider what we are saying here. How can our world change without us taking some kind of action? How are our lives going to be any different without us doing something different? **We simply cannot go on being the way we are right now and expect our world to change magically.**

Let's take the example of Joe. Joe is a nice guy but he does not have much confidence when it comes to social situations. Joe feels that most women are not interested in going out with him because in his mind he is average looking and not very interesting. Women are picking up on Joe's low opinion of himself, which shows on his face. Joe is actually putting himself at a disadvantage. As long as Joe feels this way, he is hurting his chances with romantic relationships and he probably doesn't even realize it. What would it take for Joe's situation to change?

Molly would like to go out for the basketball team but she feels that she does not measure up. Molly has talent but she lacks confidence. She is overly concerned about what other people thing about her. She is afraid that if she did not make the team that it would be a fate worse than death. So Molly holds herself back from going out for the team. What would it take for Molly's world to change?

Actually, many of us are like Joe and Molly. We actually hold ourselves back from pursuing our dreams. We may think that life is unfair or that other people are getting all the breaks when the truth is: **There is much that all of us can do to make our lives better.** When we begin to honestly realize that to a large degree we are holding ourselves back, we can begin to act differently.

We are going to consider how we can raise our levels of confidence, courage, self-esteem, and awareness throughout this book. At this point, just becoming aware that we may need to make some changes is an excellent start. We are going to have an exciting journey. Think about the rewards that await you if you will take some time to examine your life.

The Third Reason Why
Life Challenges Us

The last reason why things are the way they are is because we live in a dangerous world.

When I was a teenager in southwest Georgia, some friends and I were exploring a place called the Little Grand Canyon. I was trying to climb out of the canyon by scaling a very steep wall. I got as far as a ledge about 15 feet from the top of the canyon and realized that I could go no farther. The ledge was very small and I could hardly hang on. No one above me could seem to reach me and I just knew I was going to die. Ultimately, somehow I was rescued.

Practically anything we do is risky, but that's not a reason not to do it. Participating in sports can be perilous. Driving to work is hazardous. Getting along with certain kinds of people can be precarious. Think about how many wars have been fought on Earth. Consider how some people are so fanatical that they terrorize other people. Reflect on all the diseases there are.

If we want to live more exciting lives, we should plan on taking some risks and accepting the fact that life is unpredictable. **Many of us desire to know for certain that everything is going to be alright, but as long as we live on Earth, nothing can be guaranteed.**

We learn the most from life through direct experience. **The creator made life unpredictable so that we could learn from it.** If the world were totally safe, we would learn very little. People who always play it safe are not going to receive the kinds of rewards in life as the people who take some risks. We have to be willing to get our feelings hurt through rejection. We need to step out and try to concentrate our energy into such actions as seeing ourselves in a better way. We need to be realistic about our lives and realize that if we continue down the same road we are on nothing is going to change. **The whole purpose of this book is to help us see that we are only going to pass through this life one time, so we should do our best to live the grandest life possible.**

QUESTIONS TO PONDER

- In what ways are the people in your life predictable?

- Do you think they are ever going to change drastically?

- Would it be more realistic for you to make some changes in your life or to wait for the people in your life to change?

- If you acted with more confidence and courage, would your life be more exciting and interesting?

- Is it healthy for you to keep feeling down or depressed because other people are the way they are?

- How would your life change if you **truly believed** in your own uniqueness?

- Could you possibly be holding yourself back in life because of your opinion of yourself?

- How might your life change if you took even some small risks?

CHAPTER THREE

The Eight Great Dangers of Life

What holds us back from reaching higher levels of satisfaction in life? What holds us back from changing and becoming the people we know we are capable of being? Why do so many of us stay the way we are rather than taking steps to make our lives better?

There are eight great dangers in life that hold us back from reaching higher levels of self-fulfillment. We should focus on conquering these dangerous attitudes. These attitudes are not easy to overcome because they are ingrained into our psyche. In many cases, we may not even realize that we have attitudes that are holding us back. For example, a person who has learned to always be down on himself has to become aware of just how his attitude is hurting his chances for living a successful and meaningful life. He must somehow come to believe in his own value and self-worth--if we could just tell people that they need to act differently, everyone would change into people who live meaningful lives.

In the following pages, we are going to discuss the eight great dangerous attitudes of life. I encourage you to keep an open mind and see if you possibly fall into one or more of the categories. The truth is, all of us are guilty of some of the attitudes. If you really want to live a more rewarding life, be honest with yourself as you go through this chapter.

1. Being So Down On Ourselves That We Don't Care What Happens To Us

Some of us feel that we are average or below average people. Maybe we feel that other people are smarter, better looking, wealthier, or more accomplished, and that we really do not matter very much. Perhaps we get so down on ourselves that we don't care what happens to us. Maybe we feel hopeless. When we are down on ourselves, we are not putting our best foot forward.

Here is where the author of self-help books like this one will usually say, "it is important to focus on realizing our true value and to realize how unique we really are." Then, we say, "yeah, sure" and we put our book down and never pick it up again. I know because I have stopped reading many books. When someone tells us that we are significant, we don't believe it. We can't believe it because we have been down on ourselves for so long. In some cases, we have been down so long that being down feels natural. When we are told that we are precious human beings with priceless value, it does not make sense. It does not compute!

I want to encourage you to try and come up for air again. Stop concentrating on your past. The only place the past really exists is in your mind. Focus on not worrying so much about what other people think about you. You are an individual on this planet and you matter very much no matter what anyone tells you. You have value and worth. Other people may have convinced you that you do not matter very much. But the real problem is **you believe that you do not matter.**

It is critically important that you change your beliefs about yourself. One of the biggest mistakes we make is allowing other people to determine **how we feel about ourselves.** Thousands of people go to their graves having lived lackluster lives because the *people around them* did not tell them that they were very special.

It is **your life** that is at stake here. The way you see yourself is going to determine how many friends you have, how much money you make, how much you accomplish in life, how good your romantic life is, how well you raise your children, how meaningful your life becomes, and how long you live. Do you really want to hold yourself back from having all the joys that life has to offer? Please stop reading and answer that question, because it is an important question.

No one can make us change. We stand at the crossroads of life every day. We have to go one direction or another. One way is the familiar way, the way that we have become accustomed to going—and we know what kind of life we will lead. Taking a new road is risky, but it also offers the best chance of making our dreams come true.

When we get to a point where we don't care much about ourselves, we are treading on dangerous ground. We are more apt to abuse ourselves and to let others use and abuse us. We are more apt to make serious errors in judgment. We are more apt to put ourselves in predicaments that we don't want to be in.

Don't spend your life being down on yourself. I spent over 30 years being down on myself, and I regret it everyday of my life. I can now look back on over 50 years of living and see that being down on ourselves is a waste of time. You get one chance at life--please don't throw it away.

2. Allowing Ourselves To Get So Caught Up Into The Problems And Trials Of Life That We Forget To Live

For many of us, life is just one big problem. Some of us have never really learned how to live because we have spent our lives solving problems. We run from one crisis to the next. We often feel that our problems are worse than other people's problems. **But life is not a problem; it is an experience.** Living here on Earth is a matter of perspective.

Some people wake up in the morning and look forward to seeing what is going to happen that day. They have a natural curiosity about life because they know how fascinating it is. Others wake up and dread the day. They see life as a burden from which there is no escape.

We may have a tendency to see our existence from a limited point of view. We may feel that what happens to us is the most important thing in the world. While it is true that we need to take care of our families and ourselves, we sometimes do not see how our lives are *connected* to everyone else on the planet. I am sure that every person who has ever lived has thought that his or her problems were the most important at times. But what is life really all about? If we spend our lives solving problems, we may forget to really live.

I have problems, but I do not consider my problems to be my total life. I enjoy traveling, reading, going to movies, and spending time with my family. I also spend a lot of time reflecting on the meaning of life. Why are we here? What is the best way to spend our time while we are here? What does it all mean? Why are people the way they are?

Some of us hold ourselves back from living more rewarding lives because we are so tied up with our problems and trials. We forget to reflect, to search for true meaning in life, to pursue our dreams, and to encourage others. I am not saying that our problems are not real. I am making the point that if we are lost in solving our problems, there is no time left to live.

Anything that fills our minds completely keeps us from thinking about and pursuing other ideas, goals, and dreams. The danger here is that we may be missing tremendous opportunities and rewards because our minds are not **tuned in** to the world around us. It's not so much that concentrating on our problems is a bad thing, just that we do not leave time for other important aspects of our lives.

3. Becoming So Busy That We End Up Just Passing Time

The trials and problems of life are not the only things that consume our time. Many of us also are busy with other activities. We pursue so many activities that we don't realize our lives are getting away from us. We forget that our time here on Earth is limited. We forget that each day we are getting older and that we will not always be the same people we are right now.

Let's be honest. All of us are basically aware of how busy we have become. We want to do everything there is to be done. We want to do more and have more. But are we taking any time to improve ourselves? Are we taking time to encourage and help others? Are we trying to reach our true potential? Are we improving our spiritual selves?

I have noticed that many people are enjoying life but they are not *growing*. I believe that the reason we are here is to help others and to become the people that we have the potential to be. This does not mean that we cannot have a good time, but it does mean that having a good time is not the main reason for being here.

Prosperity and pleasure can be deceitful. **When everything is good, life does not test us as much.** We have a tendency to enjoy our prosperity and pleasure to the utmost. But sometimes our pleasures block the time we need for reflection, spiritual renewal, goal setting, and dreaming.

The great danger here is that we may be so busy with life's pleasures that all we are doing is just passing time. Again, it's a matter of perspective. What do we want out of life? If we were at the end of our lives looking back, would we be satisfied with the lives we lived?

Each of us needs to examine our lives to see if we are going in the direction we want to be going. We do not want to come to the end of our lives and to realize that we forgot to live.

4. Not Realizing That If We Are Unhappy With Our Lives, We Need To Make Some Changes

The world does not change; we change. If we are not happy, life is telling us that we need to make some changes. There is no need to waste time thinking that everything is just going to work out automatically. Things do not work out by chance; **we make things work out**.

We may think that we will somehow become more confident as we get older. We may think that people will just start being nice to us. We may feel that we will "evolve" into the kind of person we want to be. Maybe we will win the lottery. Maybe Mr. or Ms. Right is just going to waltz into our lives. Maybe someday we will just somehow "develop" more confidence and self-esteem.

If we want more of the fun rewards of life, we will need to focus on making some changes in our lives. Nothing is going to happen automatically. If we want this book to be of value, we need to understand that last statement. Until we understand that very little happens by chance, we will continue traveling the same road.

What kind of changes are we talking about? Well, we may need to develop more confidence, improve our self-concept, develop a better attitude, become more spiritual, lose weight, become more interesting, get a better education, become involved in sports, develop a sense of humor, be more positive, take some risks, worry less, or be less concerned about what others think about us. The list of changes we can make goes on and on. The important thing right now is to realize that if we are not content, **we need to do something different, because if we don't make some changes, nothing in our lives is going to change.**

The great danger here is waiting for life to make us happy. **Life is not going to make us happy. We make ourselves happy.**

We also don't know how life is going to play out. There is a very strong possibility that life will not happen the way you think it will. Be ready for lots of surprises. Factor in your own mistakes. Various circumstances are going to send your life in different directions. There are so many variables: the different kinds of people we meet, the deaths of loved ones, the mistakes we make that we had not counted on, the economy, nature, and a million other factors. Be open-minded and flexible to life's possibilities and you won't get knocked off track so easily.

For example, if you are driving and suddenly there is a car in your lane coming right at you, do you need to make a change? If your football team is behind 35-0 at halftime, is there a possibility that you need to make some changes with your team? If your doctor tells you that your health is going downhill, is there a chance that you may need to make some changes? If people in general are not responding to you in adequate ways, do you think there is a remote possibility that you might need a little self-improvement? If romantic interests do not respond to you positively, could you stand to do a little introspection? If you are not satisfied with life, is there a chance that you might need to make some changes in *yourself*?

If we can become aware that happiness, contentment, and a meaningful life are not going to fall into our laps, we will have made tremendous strides toward not throwing our lives away.

5. Not Pursuing Wisdom—Feeling That We Have It All Figured Out

I have learned that nobody has life completely figured out. One of the greatest mistakes that people make is thinking that they know how things are and how things should be. Whenever I meet someone who has all the answers, I am very skeptical of that person.

Some people feel that the way they see life is the only way life can be. In many cases, these people won't even listen to reasonable arguments to the contrary. Why? Because people largely operate out of self-interest.

People make decisions based more on self-interest than reason. For example, consider politicians who believe that only they can be right about the issues. Think about lawyers who will do anything to defend their clients no matter what the facts of the case are. What about people who deceive others with fine sounding arguments so they can get their own needs met? What about marketing companies who convince us that we have got to buy their products or our lives will be lacking? Contemplate countries who believe that going to war is in their best interest.

If we mislead ourselves or others through selfishness, through thinking we know all the answers, or through just plain ignorance, we will not be true to ourselves or others. We will end up living a self-absorbed existence and we will be walking on the edge missing true success in life.

There are great dangers in thinking that we know all the answers to life. We shut out other possibilities. We become intolerant of other people.

But we don't know how we are going to feel about the ideas or issues when we get older. We may be deceiving ourselves and other people simply because it's convenient for our lifestyle, even if it's not reasonable.

Wise people seek wisdom for as long as they live. They realize that life is very complex and that the pursuit of wisdom is a lifetime goal. They are careful not to compromise the truth by living and making decisions based only on self-interest. They realize that they cannot know all the secrets of life.

6. Not Developing The Confidence And Courage To Pursue An Exciting Life

We can have what we want in life. It is possible, but it takes confidence and courage. We don't have to be some kind of superhero. We just need to have enough basic confidence and courage to stand up for ourselves, respecting ourselves enough to believe that we deserve the rewards of life just as much as anyone else.

Sometimes we may get down on ourselves because other people make us feel that we are less than we are. This is one reason we lack confidence and courage. The truth is, **all** of us matter very much. It takes all of us to make to make the world a better place. For example, if all of us were doctors, who would teach our children? If all of us were farmers, who would take care of us when we are sick? **Every one of us matters very much.**

It is extremely important that you and I take pride in who we are and what we do. It is important to believe in our hearts that we matter. We only live one time. One of the main reasons we do not have confidence and courage is that we don't value ourselves enough.

7. Not Thinking

People who do not think about life allow life to surprise them. These people do not reflect on the human condition, therefore they fail to think ahead. They are self-absorbed, so when life throws them a curve, they are knocked off balance.

If we feel that we already have life figured out, and we do not allow the wisdom of other people to influence us, how are our lives going to turn out?

8. Being Unwilling To See Ourselves As We Really Are

A major reason why many of us hold ourselves back from living life to the fullest is because of our unwillingness to see ourselves as we really are. We tend to think that the way we are is "just the way we are supposed to be." We often do not think enough about *what we could become*.

To help us see this idea more clearly, let's look at some characters from Ayn Rand's great novel, *Atlas Shrugged*. Rand's novel is about a few movers and shakers who are the motor of the world. These people include industrialists, inventors, scientists, and shrewd business people. The novel asks the question--what happens when these prime movers go on strike? How is everyone else who is dependent on the movers affected? Rand shows how the world is moved by the creators and how other people's spirits, motives, and actions are affected when the creators cease to be involved in the affairs of the world.

Rand does an excellent job describing the characters in the novel, and in describing them, she helps us understand ourselves. For example, Dagney Taggert is the brilliant business woman who makes the major decisions for a large corporation. Her error is being overly optimistic and thinking that men are better than they are. She mistakenly believes that most people are capable of reason and that they will just somehow become enlightened.

Then there is Hank Reardon, the steel industrialist. His main flaw is his willingness to be convinced by the wrong people that he must serve others. Reardon struggles with misconceptions about himself that keep him from seeing his own greatness. Hank's wife Lillian, is a beautiful but lifeless woman. She is full of contempt for her husband and his capacity to make a lot of money--and thereby have the power in the family.

James Taggert, another executive, manipulates the system. He claims to be motivated by public service but his true motives are to destroy others. Jim is weak and dependent on public opinion for every decision he makes.

Then there is John Galt who is strong, confident and shrewd. He deals directly with objective facts and though he is ruled by reason, he is able to express his emotions as well. Much of the economic success of the world revolves around him.

Rand describes Galt as being man in his ideal form. Galt also represents the theme of the novel, the idea that the mind is the power that drives civilization.

These characters are prototypes to help us see that we all view the world in certain ways, and that we may find it hard to see ourselves as we really are. **If we are unable to see ourselves as we are, we are obviously destined to make a lot of mistakes and poor choices.**

If we can see our **real selves**, not the people we have learned to be, we can accomplish grander goals and find much more meaning in life. Abraham Lincoln, Dr. Martin Luther King Jr, President John F. Kennedy, Robert Kennedy,

Mother Teresa and many others made significant contributions to society. These people found meaning in helping others, and they worked to make the world a better place to live. But if they had not spent some time **contemplating** their lives, **improving** themselves, and **reaching** for higher purposes, we may have never heard of them. We may not be able to influence people on such a large scale as these people, but we can help others in our part of the world.

QUESTIONS TO PONDER

- What is going to happen to us if we go through life not caring what happens to us?

- Could we be so busy with the problems and challenges of life that we are not leaving any room to really enjoy life?

- Is it possible that we could be so busy running from one activity to another that we do not realize what life is really all about? Are we growing mentally and spiritually?

- If we are not as happy as we would like to be, do we need to consider making some changes in our lives?

- If we "hold back" in life and do not develop more confidence and courage, can we expect to live the most rewarding life possible?

CHAPTER FOUR

Is it You, God, or Fate?

What we need the most in this life is for someone to tell us the truth. Here is one of the main truths: **very few situations are going to come into our lives that we don't cause to happen.** Once we learn and understand this idea, we can move forward with our lives. Learn it! Memorize it! It is the most important concept in life!

Every day can be a heartache if we are playing the waiting game: waiting for that certain person to call, waiting for that promotion, waiting until the time is right to write that book, waiting for a raise, waiting to win the lottery, waiting to lose weight, and waiting for circumstances to get better so that we can take certain actions. Waiting for something to happen is a kind of dream state that we allow ourselves to fall into.

Let's consider some questions to help us understand this important point. If you want to be with a man or woman right now, do you need to take some kind of action? If you want more money right now, do you need to take some kind of action? If you want to write a book or a song, do you need to take some kind of action? If you want to be a super athlete, do you need to take some kind of action? As you can see, **action** is the key. We will get more of what we want when we **believe**

that taking action is what makes things happen. Period.

Intentions, though they may be the grandest imaginable, will get us nowhere if we do not take action. We may *intend* to accomplish certain goals before we die. We may *intend* to improve our relationships, get a handle on our anger, lose weight, or improve our self-image, but without action, our goals are only intentions. When we take action, something has to happen.

Do not wait for fate or God to make your dreams come true. **You make your dreams come true.** Success, romance, money, and excitement are not going to come without effort. Your own actions are going to bring you the greatest rewards, at least here on earth.

Don't Ever Give Up

It takes a certain strength and diligence to continue taking action in life and not give up. If we can just hang in there a while longer, there is usually light around the corner. Our degree of diligence actually makes us who we are. Sometimes life can be so utterly frustrating. Other people seem to get all the breaks. We may feel totally inadequate. Life can seem so unfair at times.

Still, we must push on, because no matter how bad life may seem, nothing is going to happen **magically**. There is no mystical force that is going to make our life become the meaningful existence that we would like for it to be.

It is very easy to give up and live an average life. **Life is a really, really demanding experience.** And if life does not seem to be demanding much of us, chances are we may not be living a very full life. Let's consider Paula's situation.

Paula's Precarious Predicament

Paula was a smart and popular woman who had big plans. She wanted to write a book. She also wanted to be a singer. In addition, she wanted to get married and have a family. Unfortunately, Paula had big plans but no drive.

She had been talking about writing her book for three years. She had written a few pages but she seemed to be waiting until she could write words that were utterly perfect and profound. She was waiting for the muse to come over her so that she would feel wonderful as she wrote.

Paula also had a lovely voice, but she could hardly ever find the time to practice. She was overly involved in trivial activities such as watching too much television, surfing the internet, and attending as many events as possible. But Paula kept telling herself that "one day" she was going to be a great and well-known singer.

As far as romance, Paula was looking for a man who was perfect. She set her standards so high that nobody could meet them. When she did meet nice guys they could sense that Paula desired more than they could offer. Paula pushed guys away without realizing it because she had a hard time loosening up.

Time was the great equalizer in life. Paula's life slowly passed by and she never wrote a book, never developed her voice, and she never got married. She began to get a little age on her, which made pursuing her goals more difficult. She had less energy and sometimes she did not feel well. Compared with her dreams, her average life made her become hardened and sometimes depressed. Life was not as fun, rewarding, and as exciting as it had been because Paula thought she had life figured out when she was younger.

All of us can relate to Paula's story. **All of us have dreams that did not come true because we waited for the right time, the perfect moment, the heavenly inspiration, the perfect words to say, or the unattainable man or woman.** So we grew older and resentful of life because it did not work out the way we just knew it would. Now it may be too late to pursue some of our goals. We may be in Paula's predicament.

Now Is The Time To Live

There is no perfect moment; there is only now. Some moments will be better than others. **Those who wait on life to make them happy are going to be disappointed.**

You did not ask to be born. You had no choice or any say about the kind of family you were born into. The way you were raised is the only way you knew. If your parents were down on themselves, you probably have a tendency to be down on yourself. You probably had some negative experiences somewhere in your past that are affecting the way you experience life now. Perhaps a teacher put you down. Maybe a close friend betrayed you or treated you badly. Possibly someone hurt your feelings or hurt you physically. The point is: these negative moments are affecting the way you experience life *right now*. It is up to you to take an active role in your own life and to start seeing the real you. **No matter where you were born, the person that you become will be determined by how strong your desire is to overcome your shortcomings and limitations.**

You do not have to accept the life you are now living as the only life possible for you. You have the power to **shape** your life. Reflect on what I am saying. Life is an amazing experience, but we must get past the limited way that we may be looking at it. You and I need to see the fullness of being human. Our potential goes way beyond the way we see ourselves at the moment. I guarantee it. We are amazing creatures! The possibilities within us are absolutely endless. But too often we don't take the time to see the true miracles that we are. We let our circumstances and emotions control us.

We only get to go through life one time. Are we reaching for the golden ring and creating an exciting adventure-- or just passing time?

We just happen to be living at this point in history, but when we were born is not nearly as important as trying to make something of our lives. We are living, breathing beings with incredible minds! Focus on seeing the *you* that you dream about. Decide once and for all that you are not going to let circumstances, other people, and your own limited view of yourself to keep holding you back from being the person **you know you can be**.

You and I are creating our lives from moment to moment. We will **never** pass this way again. Please examine your life. What do you want to do with your life? What are you going to do for others? Whatever your answer is will be your destiny. If you are satisfied now, you will be basically the same person 20 years from now. If you want to make some changes now, you will be a different person in 20 years. **It's all up to you. It is not fate; it is you.**

We need to appreciate our lives **right now**. Recently I visited a friend of mine in the Intensive Care Unit of a local hospital. He looked so bad that I was shocked. Only two weeks before he had told me that his doctors were going to perform a heart catherization. Unfortunately, things did not go well, so he had open-heart surgery. After a few days, the doctor had to open his chest again. The doctors said he was lucky to be living.

I am not even sure that my friend recognized me. He had a stunned look on his face and a tube down his throat as big as a water hose.

Please don't put off living a richer, more fulfilling life-- you don't know what is ahead for you. I really don't mean to sound so negative, but if you had seen my friend you would know just how lucky you are to have this opportunity, today, to change your life.

Can We Really Transform Our Lives?

It is a fact that most people who are in prison have a poor self-concept. Their poor self-concept has caused them to make unwise choices. Actually, any of us who do not feel positive about ourselves will make many unwise choices, but so far perhaps we have managed to stay out of prison. But anytime we hold ourselves back by being down on ourselves, we still put ourselves in a sort of mental prison.

The beginning of making sense of life is for us to see ourselves as **significant human beings.** If we are not able to comprehend our inestimable value as individuals, we will not be motivated to alter our lives for the better.

How do we change? This is the million-dollar question. For centuries, people have argued about whether we are simply destined to be the way we are or whether we are actually capable of transforming our lives. **We do not have the time or the luxury to consider ourselves incapable of becoming the people we are capable of being—obviously we can change.** Just look around at people who have made significant shifts in their lives. **We don't need to waste time thinking that we can't transform our lives. We must move on.**

The first step in transforming ourselves is **believing that change is possible**. We are not destined to be the way we are. **There is no mysterious power holding us back.** If we become more confident now, we will get more of the rewards and prizes of life.

Try to remove any thoughts and feelings that may hinder our communication. I am reaching out to you as a friend. You know me only through this book, but I care what happens to you.

Are you really happy or do you often struggle with life? What do you really long for? Do you struggle dealing with yourself, other people, or strange thoughts? Do you feel unfulfilled? How many times have you searched for the answers to the mysteries in your life? How many times have you been disillusioned?

I am telling you that you can discover meaning in your life. It's not easy to grab hold of the golden ring--if it were, everyone would do it. Finding significance is more than just following a list of rules or guidelines. **It is a journey of self-discovery.**

One way I can help you is by letting you know the substantial changes I have made in my own life. I have wrestled with alcohol, drugs, strange thoughts, fantasies, and low self-esteem. But I have also found much contentment, and my message to **you is that you can overcome whatever is holding you back. You can overcome anything.**

I feel compelled to share my message with you. In one 100 years, you and I will not even be alive. If we are not living an exhilarating and meaningful life **right now**, we are throwing away our one shot at life!

QUESTIONS TO PONDER

- Why do so many people feel the need to "escape" from life?

- Do we have the time and the luxury to go through life believing we are incapable of changing? How does what we believe shape our future?

- How can we learn to feel special, valuable, wanted, and needed?

- What would it take to feel that we are uniquely individual and that we have something special to offer the world?

- Is there a mysterious force holding us back from living more exciting lives--or could we be holding ourselves back?

CHAPTER FIVE

Be Young, Foolish, and Happy

When I was 12 years old, I fell in love with the cutest girl in the world. I could hardly wait for each new day so that I could see her again. She did not feel the same as I did, but still, getting to be around her was exhilarating and she brought a lot of excitement into my life.

As we go through life, we can lose the sense of excitement and adventure that we once had by allowing negative situations to bring us down. **We were not meant to go through life being disillusioned.** Think about how happy most babies are. They have not yet learned to worry, or be afraid, or to feel down on themselves. Life is just one big exciting experience.

As we grow older, we have to deal with people and cope with challenging circumstances. We quickly learn that some people are nicer than others, and that some people like to put other people down. We begin to realize that people play a lot of mind games. Some people have more money than others. Some people think they are better than other people. We come to understand that we have our limitations.

Whatever the case, **we live in reality**. This is not a movie.

49

It does not take us long to realize that nobody can follow us around and fight our battles for us. **We have to interact with others. We have to learn how to act to get along with others. We have to do something. Completely avoiding people is impossible.**

Along the way, we develop our personalities. The way we act and behave is partly inherited. The way that our parents and friends treat us also plays a major role in the development of our personalities. **But once we have developed our personalities, are we locked into those behaviors like robots? Do we have no control over our lives?**

Some people respond to the world by withdrawing, being standoffish, and avoiding people. Some people learn to feel down on themselves. Other people start escaping from the world through alcohol and drugs.

The bottom line is that we have to learn to deal with the world. We cannot hide away in a closet. **When we come to realize and believe that we really do have power, we can really begin living.**

Somewhere Along The Way We Got Off Track

Please consider very carefully what I am going to say to you. Being mean, stuck-up, hateful, egotistical, withdrawn, standoffish, depressed, and so on, are various phases that we go through as humans. **It is critically important to understand that if we do not change our behaviors as we grow up, we will turn into adults who are mean, stuck-up, hateful, egotistical, standoffish, or depressed.** This is how older people get to be the way they are—**they don't change.**

When we don't try hard enough to improve ourselves, we basically stay the same. We allow our feelings and the people and events around us to determine how we feel. **Instead of creating an exciting life of our own, we let life create us.** Life itself ends up determining how we feel and what happens to us.

What Is The Answer?

Try to understand that it is the way we think about ourselves and the events in our lives that determine how we experience life. **The secret of living a more fun and meaningful life is realizing that we are in control.** Other people and events are not our lives; they are just things in our lives.

We really should look forward to each new day as if we were all 12-year-olds in love. Life is an experience to cherish. But, many of us get knocked off track somewhere along the way, and we just never do get back in the game. We let life get to us. People hurt our feelings. We fail to live up to our own expectations. Unexpected events knock us off balance.

As I said earlier, please try to understand that life is not going to turn out exactly the way we've planned. Life can be a really strange experience. Some experiences will take us to the mountaintop and others will take us into the depths of despair. We are going to meet some people who seem to be angels and others who seem to be demons. Many times life will not seem fair. Life is complicated and sometimes very difficult to understand. **But the key is not letting other people and events control our lives.**

We need to be happy right now. **To be otherwise is simply a waste of time.** We can waste our 80 or so years on earth worrying. We can exhaust our time being down on ourselves and feeling sorry for ourselves. We can squander our time trying to escape or thinking we are only average people. But all of these negative thoughts are basically **a waste of time**. How many good times are we missing right now?

Focus on being more confident and courageous. Concentrate on looking your very best and being an interesting person. Walk tall and put some pep in your step. Believe in your own uniqueness.

Other people do not determine your value as a person. What do they know? Other people have their own agendas. Making you feel happy is not foremost in their minds. I don't mean to sound harsh or mean-spirited. It's just that if you and I are ever going to move forward, we have got to realize that we need to take care of ourselves and stop giving people power over us. **We create our own world.**

Make your life happen!

Living Life In The Long Term

As we live life from day to day, we can easily forget that time is steadily moving on. We can get caught up in the pleasures of the moment and think only of the here and now. We may give value to ourselves based on the perception that we have of ourselves at the present moment. For example, we may base our total meaning and contributions to life based on our present level of strength, knowledge, influence, social status, and physical attributes.

But the present moment is only a tiny piece of the puzzle of life. You and I are constantly changing so we can give more realistic value to the moments of our lives by realizing that we are changing. For example, we may look down on or resent certain other people because they do not share our values at this moment, even though at some future point in time, we may feel completely different. We may look down on people who are less fortunate than us who we feel "should be doing better." On the other hand, we may look up to others or put others on a pedestal who really are not much smarter than we are, simply because we stand on shaky ground with our own beliefs, self-images, perceptions, and philosophies.

If the experience that we are having right now isn't flexible, we may develop attitudes that limit our understanding and enjoyment of life. If we are intolerant of other people because they don't see life the way we do, we may have very few friends. Our life meaning will be based totally on our own perceptions.

But the laws of life are going to hold true whether we are right or wrong. It is helpful to see situations as learning experiences rather than random happenings that hold no meaning whatsoever. Most of us do not hold the truths of life as much as we think we do. Or if we feel that only we hold the truth we may be deceiving ourselves.

Living a meaningful life involves growing as a person. We cannot grow if we stay the same. We should focus more on **interpreting** the events that come our way in light of our purpose for existing rather than just **reacting** to all that is going on around us. When we are only reacting to people and situations, we are not coming to an understanding of ourselves. We are not becoming the best that we can be.

Remember that time is slowly slipping away. **When we come to realize that what happens to us really is up to us, we will start seeing life differently.** When it dawns on us that we have real power and influence, our lives will take on new meaning.

I do not want you to believe what I say just because I say it. Use what works for you.

Making Sense Of Our Existence

Marcy, Jana and Lauren all grew up in the same town. Marcy was pretty and she grew up in a wealthy, educated family. She got a college degree and married a wealthy, influential man who she met at college. The couple had two lovely children. As Marcy lived out her life, she saw herself as a wealthy, educated person and she chose to do activities that wealthy, educated people do. Though she had everything money could buy, she often felt that she was just going through the motions in her life.

Jana grew up in a middle-income family. The family members saw themselves as average people. They were blue-collar workers and they did not pursue college degrees. Jana learned to see herself as an average girl and often felt that she had to try harder to compete with girls like Marcy. Jana wore her jeans two sizes too small and drank too much. She married a guy who was a blue-collar worker and she got an average job. She and her husband had two children who learned to feel that they were average people.

Lauren grew up in a low-income family. She often felt that she was not as good as other people. Lauren tried to overcompensate for her shortcomings by wearing sexy clothes and dabbling in drugs and alcohol. She did not see much of a future for herself so she did not consider going to college. Lauren saw herself as unlucky and unfortunate. She ended up marrying a guy who she ultimately had to divorce because of all the arguing and fighting over money and various other problems. Lauren and her husband had three children who have low self-esteem.

All three of these women learned to see themselves in certain ways based on the kind of surroundings they grew up in. The same thing happens to all of us. **We learn to see ourselves and the world in a certain way.** Since we only get one chance at life, it is helpful to try and see ourselves in a different or more positive way.

To live a more meaningful life, we need to see ourselves as being more than the people we were raised to be. Too often, we play the roles we think we are supposed to play. We should focus on seeing ourselves as people who are equal to other people, not less than or better than anyone else.

If we feel we are **destined** to be a certain way, we don't try to change. Many of our actions and behaviors are simply **habits. We go through life never realizing our tremendous potential waiting to be unleashed. We can't see the possibilities in our lives because we are living out our "script."**

Our lives are like movies already planned out. Other people have convinced us that we are great, average, stupid, ugly, attractive, smart or dumb. To live a more meaningful life, we must **break our habitual, learned behaviors.** We have to create a sequel to our movie.

Do we *really* have the potential to change, you might be asking? Does a bully **have** to push people around? Does a cashier at a hamburger stand **have** to stay at that job forever? Do people **have** to be sad all the time? Do people **have** to be shy or could they possibly change? Do people **have** to take drugs and drink alcohol? Do some people **have** to go through life with low self-esteem or a poor self-concept? Do people **have** to go through life thinking that life is a miserable experience? Do people **have** to spend their lives blaming everybody else for the condition of the world? **Is it simply impossible for all these people to make some changes in their lives?**

To make sense of life and to find more meaning, we have got to get past the idea that we are **just destined to be who we are. This idea or thought is holding us back.** Please stop reading for a moment and think about that. I want to turn on a light in your head that will help you see that you and I hold *ourselves* back from being happier and living more meaningful lives.

My friend, why did Marcy, Jana, and Lauren live the kind of lives I described? What would have happened to Lauren if she had been raised by Marcy's wealthy and educated parents? What if Marcy had been raised by Lauren's poor parents? Do you think there is a possibility that Marcy would have low self-esteem? Here is the point: **It really does not matter how we were raised. It is what we do with what we have that matters.** If we were raised by parents who had low self-esteem, we need to wake up and work on developing a better self-image. We need to overcome the idea that we are destined to be the way we are or the idea that some strange force is keeping us where we are.

Do We Really Want To Change?

Even if you are beginning to accept what I am saying, there is a possibility that you may not want to change. Let's think about this for a moment.

Too often, we allow uncomfortable thoughts to rob us of

our joy. If we do not change the kinds of thoughts we have, they will stay with us for a lifetime. The following is a list of the kind of thoughts that take our joy from us:

"Other people are smarter than I am."

"Other people are physically and emotionally stronger than I am."

"Girls (Guys) do not pay attention to me."

"I cannot lose weight."

"What if I say or do the wrong thing and someone confronts me?"

"What if I look bad in front of others?"

"What if I fail?"

"It's just another ordinary day."

"Life is humdrum."

"Other people are more important than I am."

These types of thoughts are **emotionally crippling.** They hold us back in every area of our lives--socially, economically, romantically, and mentally. It is odd that even if we realize how much these thoughts are hurting us, we still continue having them. What does this tell us?

It tells us that we are determined not to change. Even though we think we are miserable in our present state, we may actually like the way we are more than we realize. Our thoughts have become a sort of refuge for us. In other words, we are able to escape into our thoughts about how bad things are, and this way we can justify the way we are.

Let's look more closely at what I am saying. Do we really want to change? For example, if we become more appealing by becoming more fun to be around, there are always consequences. When we attract a man or a woman, that person expects us to perform. They are trying to have fun and find meaning also. But if we are boring or not very interesting, the relationship will not last long, and the pressure will be off. **Rather than have too much expected of us, we might rather stay the way we are.**

Let's go farther. Anytime we become more confident, other people expect more from us. This is true with our jobs, families, and all other social situations. **We need to ask ourselves if we really want to change.**

The simple truth of the matter may be that we are happier than we think we are. **After reading this book, you will either strive to live a more fulfilling life or you will understand why you are staying the way you are.** There really is no middle ground. Either we are living a life based on our limited awareness of life, or we are trying to raise our level of awareness.

We only get one shot at life. Is the life you are living the only one possible for you? Is there no other way to look at your life? Is it impossible for you to make some changes?

The years pass by and many people never come to understand that **it is not what's going on around us that is important, but what we are doing with the abilities that we have.**

Your Story

Each day is another chance to improve your aim and live a fun, meaningful, and exciting life. **There are no ordinary days.** Everyday has meaning, purpose, and significance. Life does not just happen; we play a major role in our own story.

We have the possibility to write a new script daily. Each day that we are alive is another chance to do better, reach higher, feel better, meet new people, develop better friendships, improve our self-esteem, have exciting feelings, and to help other people. You and I are writing our own story every day.

What is a day? A day is your movie "set." A day is the physical environment in which you live out your story. In your movie there are all kinds of people and situations. **It is not these people and situations that determine what happens to you, but the way you interact with these people and situations.** Again, we are helping you to see **you are in control of your life.**

Take Sandy. Sandy was an average girl who got along with most people. But she often felt that her happiness was determined by the kind of moods other people were in each day. If other people felt good, Sandy would usually feel better. If others were down, Sandy would often feel down. For years, Sandy felt like she had little control over her world. She just did not feel complete and fulfilled.

Fortunately, Sandy came to understand that if she wanted to live a more fulfilling life, she **would need to focus on seeing herself differently.** She came to understand that making changes in her life was **up to her.** She began to truly believe in herself, and her new confidence began to show up in her face. Other people began to respond to her differently. She became happier and more appealing because she had more to offer. Her story became a happy story.

Your story can be a happy story, too. Each day is another chance to improve your aim.

QUESTIONS TO PONDER

- If we go through life feeling disillusioned, what kind of life are we going to have?

- Do we have any control over our lives or are we totally helpless?

- What kind of lives can we expect to live if we allow circumstances and other people's opinions to control us?

- Would we be better off interpreting the events in our lives as having meaning or by responding to life with knee-jerk responses?

- When people think about you, what kind of thoughts do you think they have?

- If you died today, how would people remember you?

- How would you like to be remembered?

- What actions can you take daily to cause your story to have a happy ending?

CHAPTER SIX

Ways to Find
More Meaning in Life

*E*veryone in the world is looking for some kind of meaning in their life. If you understand that last statement, you will have gained wisdom. From the oldest to the youngest, the meanest to the nicest, the richest to the poorest, everyone you meet is looking for meaning.

Some people may not realize what they are looking for. Others may have given up on finding any meaning. Still others may deny they are looking for meaning. But make no mistake about it--all of us are searching for meaning.

What is meaning? Meaning is something that makes us feel that we matter. Some people do not search diligently for meaning because they get so much attention from their looks, money, or accomplishments that they feel their lives must be meaningful, whether they really are or not. Still other people have learned to feel that their lives are not very meaningful and that they are less than adequate people. Life may have pounded them into the ground. They may feel unattractive. They may not have developed much confidence. They may not have been in a position to make much money.

The greatest tragedy on earth is for any person to feel

that he or she does not matter. I know of no sadder situation. Generation after generation, the same scenarios play out over and over. In schools, the bright, attractive children are treated better than children who may be less attractive or bright. The world gives the message to this last group of children that they don't matter as much as the other children. This is the bottom line problem with the whole world. It is the reason that many people resort to drugs and alcohol, the reason that many people commit suicide, the reason that many people don't try to go farther in their careers, and the reason that more people don't feel loved, wanted, needed, accepted, and valued.

In this section, I am going to suggest some ways to start finding meaning in life. My purpose here is not to convince you to look at life the same way I do, but to offer some possibilities that may help you live a more meaningful life. Your life matters so much more than you may realize right now, and I want to help you see the true possibilities in your life. You are a mother or father or friend or daughter or son. **You are somebody. Please make your life mean something.**

How Do We Find Meaning?

Martin Luther King, Jr. has always been one of my heroes. He helped thousands of people feel that they matter. Before he came along, many people believed that they were second-class citizens. But King knew one of the true secrets of living a meaning life: serving others. King asserted that anyone could be great by serving others, and that serving others "does not take a college degree and does not require that our subjects and verbs agree". It just takes desire.

Serving others helps us get outside of ourselves. It takes the attention off us. Obviously, some of us are not knockouts when it comes to looks. Some of us are not as smart or accomplished as others. But all of us can serve others.

Helping others has really always been an important way for us to find meaning in our lives. It's just that many people feel that pleasing themselves is more important than helping others. These people have deceived themselves into thinking that they somehow deserve as much pleasure as possible while they are on earth. The idea of serving and helping others is corny and outdated to them. Yet in the deepest recesses of their minds, they can't understand why their lives seem to lack meaning.

Serving others is one major way to see a bigger picture. We must be careful, though, that we do not spend so much time serving others that we become resentful or hardened because we are not taking time to take care of our own needs. Some people become martyrs and totally lose themselves in helping others but on the inside these people are miserable. It is very important that we take care of our own needs first.

Seeking Our Grand Purpose

Another great way to find meaning in life is by finding our purpose for being here or by creating a purpose. All of us are different and unique, from DNA to fingerprints. All of us have a unique purpose for being alive. Many people feel that they can't find their purpose but this notion is putting up a roadblock in their minds.

Our purpose for living may not come to us like a bolt of lightning. We may have to experience more of life to discover what we want to do. It is extremely important that we move forward and not become complacent. It is profitable to live active lives as we search for our purpose. We cannot know for certain how anything is going to work out. **We must take risks to live out our dreams.**

An important step we can take right now is to stop saying, "I don't know what my purpose is." This statement only holds us back from trying. If we search hard enough, we will find our purpose. Telling ourselves that we can't find our purpose is just as limiting as allowing others to control us. All of these thoughts hold us back from experiencing a meaningful life.

Find Meaning By Considering That Searching For The Meaning Of Life Is The Purpose Of Life

We may find that simply looking for the meaning of life is the meaning of life. We have marvelous minds and a natural curiosity. It is the tension within us that causes us to search for meaning in life. **We know that the tension between what we are and what we would like to be, determines what we become.** Tension is what drives us. Without this drive, we would not be motivated to seek a more rewarding existence.

We are exploring possibilities here. There are few absolutes in life. Try to be open to what we are saying and you may stumble upon the key that unlocks the door to your happiness. Remember, there is no one simple answer when it comes to finding the meaning of life. Life is very complex, but if we think through the possibilities, we may meet with surprising results and success.

Consider The Desire To Find Meaning As A Part Of Human Nature

Perhaps the desire to find meaning in life is just part of being human and it is something to be celebrated rather than something to worry about. Again, desire is what pushes us forward and makes us act. Our natural state is to search and find out who we are and why we are here. This natural desire is a wonderful part of being human. If we had no desire to push us, we would spend a lot of time making poor choices and perhaps accomplishing very little.

We really are living miracles. Just think--we don't have to think about how to raise our arm or how to walk. Too often we concern ourselves with trivial things that do not matter very much in the long run and yet fail to see the fascinating individuals we are.

Too many people spend their lives getting ready to live. They deprive themselves of daily fulfillment by postponing their happiness in favor of some future success or situation. **Life is a journey to be enjoyed now.**

Consider That Finding Meaning in Life May Not Be Necessary For Happiness

We may be able to find happiness without searching for the meaning of life. We can find tremendous happiness in **just being**. We often find a lot of joy in doing our favorite activities, enjoying our families, and recognizing how thrilling it is to be alive. Rather than a search, life can be a constant source of fulfillment.

When we accept ourselves as the unique individuals that we are, we can find much contentment in simply living. We can also find a lot of contentment by appreciating the fabulous diversity of the world. The world is an utterly fascinating place to experience.

Creating Meaning In Our Lives

Another way to live a more meaningful life is to create a meaning and purpose for our lives. Perhaps we could do volunteer work, write a book, coach a sports team, or visit the sick. Maybe we should have been doing this all the time and did not realize it. We were waiting for something to fall out of the sky and hit us on the head but it was probably never going to happen. Earlier we discussed the idea that **we cannot wait for something to happen in life.** Part of the whole experience of living is realizing that we are co-creators of our own lives.

We need a reason to wake up. We need something to keep us going. Every day we have to decide how we are going to use the day. **There has to be something to draw us forward. We should strive to be happy even in our present circumstances. Every moment of life is precious.**

We may think, for example, that the only way for us to be happy is by working in glamorous jobs such as modeling, acting, advertising, entertainment, or the media. But consider that each day thousands of men and women go to work as waiters, waitresses, clerks and laborers. There is certainly nothing wrong with these jobs and many people in these fields are quite happy.

So what brings meaning into the lives of these people? Is it having a good mate? Raising their children? Spending time with their family? Surviving? Sports? Getting high? Dreaming that things will get better? Going to movies? Do they even feel that their lives have any meaning?

It is extremely important to realize that we can create meaning in our lives from moment to moment. Every breath of life is another moment that we will never see again. When we bring meaning to other people by doing our job the best we can, by supporting our families and friends the best we can, and by constantly trying to improve ourselves and our situation, we create our own meaning.

We Can Create Meaning By Taking A Closer Look At Our Lives

Feelings and emotions are not just some strange phenomena that we must suffer. Numerous philosophers such as Aristotle, Plato, and Thomas Aquinas have asserted that emotions do not just come out of nowhere but from our unconscious mind, but the emotions are caused by the way we perceive and comprehend the world. So negative feelings and emotions can be changed by examining our lives and the way we have perceived events and circumstances.

Many of us have values and assumptions that affect our thinking more than we realize. We largely developed our thinking during childhood, and some of these thoughts may be distorted. We can come to a higher awareness of our conflicting values and mistaken certainties by being willing to examine our lives closely rather that just blindly pursuing our habitual ways.

It would be admirable for us to take a closer look at our lives because our happiness that we attain depends on how we look at the world.

Finding Meaning By
Treating Others With Love
And Kindness

Our planet has a violent history. Throughout the ages, many people have treated one another with brutality, savagery, and violence. People have often hurt others to get their own needs met. **Surely there is more to life than treating others as no more than animals.**

Loving others will bring great meaning into our lives. Rather than going through life resentful, we would do well to focus on understanding other people.

Perhaps we can even become examples of love. Love is the most precious attitude that we can have. Love will bring us life. Every act of kindness is meaningful. We would do well to love even those who don't love us. Jesus Christ said in Matthew 5:46, "If you love only those who love you, what reward do you have?"

Love is another attitude that helps us get outside of ourselves and our own problems. Everybody has problems, and a great way to find meaning is for us to share our love with humanity. It is helpful to try and understand why others are the way they are and to understand the kind of trials they may be suffering. This involves not thinking that we know all the answers to life and not feeling that we totally understand other people. It also means that we do not try to make other people be more like us.

Loving others is one of the true secrets of finding meaning in life.

Find Meaning By
Rising Above Mediocrity

When we look around, it is easy to see that many people are not living fulfilling, purposeful lives. These people blame other people and situations for their problems and they end up just getting by and not really living.

The beginning of living a more purposeful and meaningful life is realizing that if we are allowing other people or situations to control us, we are keeping ourselves in our own **mental prison. It is simply impossible to please other people all the time.** In addition, if we are concentrating on our limitations and failures, then we are not thinking enough about what we could be. Shakespeare said, "We know what we are, but not what we may be."

Only to the degree that we are able to free ourselves from our limitations and acknowledge our own uniqueness can we begin to develop the confidence to go after a more meaningful life.

Our beliefs imprison us and keep us from seeing the real truth about ourselves. If our beliefs are distorted or false, our whole way of looking at life will be distorted. How do we change our beliefs if they are not serving us well? Again, we come back to rigorous self-examination.

We will change according to the degree of truth that we can accept about ourselves.

Find Meaning By Questioning Life

Many people look at life from a short-term point of view. They do not think much about their coming death or where their journey is headed. They stay fairly content enjoying the many amusements and diversions along the way. Their lives are largely on automatic, and they live from moment to moment. They keep themselves preoccupied, so they seldom notice that their lives aren't as meaningful as they could be until something snaps them out of their habitual life style-- which leaves them empty and alone.

We can create meaning in many areas of our lives such as enjoying our families, making money, and accomplishing goals, **but we still feel empty sometimes. We need to question ourselves regularly and examine our lives closely to see if there are areas in our lives that could be improved. We may deceive ourselves if we go through life always thinking that we have "found it."** Remember, ten years from now we are not going to feel the way we do right now.

We can find great meaning by questioning ourselves rather than taking our lives for granted.

Find Meaning By Looking For The Significance Of The Events In Our Lives

Life is unbearable without meaning. Many people die within a few years after their retirement because they feel that they no longer have enough meaning in their lives. Some rich people are very unhappy for the same reason.

Life is a series of events that happen over time. Every phase of our lives is significant, from childhood to retirement. We can find meaning by turning the events in our lives into positive aspects of our lives. **The events of life make us what we become.** The way we handle the situations that come our way creates the kind of meaning we experience.

Realize That A Lot Of What Is Meaningful In Life Is Not Fun

Life is not simply about having a good time. A lot of activities that make life worth living are not fun. For example, studying hard in school, training hard for an athletic contest, and working hard at a job may not be pleasurable, but these activities ultimately help bring us meaning. Many activities in life are rewarding even though they are not fun.

Find Meaning By Realizing That The World Is A Kind Of Training Ground

Life has a scheme to it. Life has order and logic. Our creator made us in such a way that we can go in any direction that we desire. We may be attractive or unattractive, smart or not so smart, rich or poor. We are not meant to be perfect. **Our imperfections are what drive us to develop ourselves. It is the seeming unfairness of life that makes us try harder, do better, and reach for higher levels of satisfaction.**

We complain about life because we feel for some reason that life should be perfect and problem-free. It seems to us that other people are having all the fun. These feelings are just part of being alive.

Having disadvantages can push us to reach for what we want and to become what we are capable of being. Life is like a school. It is teaching us that we should improve ourselves and raise our level of awareness if we want to be happier. **But again, one mistake we make is thinking that life should be what we think it should be. Life is what it is.**

Find Meaning By Realizing That Trying To Understand Each Other Will Bring The Greatest Meaning To All Of Us

Many intelligent people feel that their way of seeing certain issues is the only way possible. They go to extremes. They assert that people who do not agree with them are ignorant or superstitious.

If we want to truly live a more meaningful life, we need to answer the following questions honestly. Do we believe in and defend our beliefs because we truly have infallible evidence and reasons, or because our beliefs suit our purposes and our egos? Could it be that we are blind to what is truly going on because of our self-righteous beliefs, whether they be in science, religion, or whatever?

If we restrict ourselves by feeling that we have all the answers, we will be ignorant of knowledge that we could have gained from other experiences. We will hold ourselves back and not even realize it. Our pride will keep us from gaining what may have been the greatest experiences of our lives. In our intolerance of others, we may become the supreme example of intolerance.

Our greatest learning comes from realizing how little we really know.

Another Secret Of Living
A Meaningful Life

People who live the most meaningful lives are people who are connected to themselves, others, the world, and the universe. **They live life on purpose.** They cause success to come into their lives and the lives of other people. Each day they plan, set goals, and **make things happen.**

They enjoy other people and do not feel the need to put them down to make themselves feel better. They make others feel good because they have a certain peace about them. They do not allow external factors such as the weather or the economy to determine whether they are happy or not.

They are inspired people. They feel a sense of purpose and destiny. They know that they have a reason for being here and they know that they matter. They inspire others. They do not feel the need to win or prove anything, therefore their lives are in harmony with the world.

They are constantly learning new things. They are thankful for life and they are humble. Because of these virtues, **they also bring much meaning into the lives of other people.**

Find Meaning By
Facing Life Head-On

As I think back over my life, I realize that I have not always been confident enough. Facing life head-on is the way to live a meaningful life. Start taking charge of your life and standing up for yourself. What happens to you—is up to you.

I was in the fight of my life a while back. During a

Taekwondo (karate) testing, I kicked an opponent in the side of his leg and I felt that I had broken my big toe. I continued the fight though I was in a lot of pain. In a minute or so, I had to move on to my next opponent--who was out for blood. He was 23 and I was 53. I was exhausted from two previous matches and I had a painful toe. It was all I could do to keep this man off me. We were in front of a large audience and I knew I had to keep going no matter what. I was able to get through the match, but I'll never forget how far I had to reach into my soul to find the willpower to keep going.

Sometimes, we have to **reach beyond** our natural abilities to win some battles and get through life. Some situations demand that we reach into the inner depths of our being to find the courage and perseverance to face them head-on.

My friend, we must face life realistically if we are going to be happy. **Please don't live in a fantasy world of wishful thinking. We are in control of our lives.**

Life is fantastic! Spend some time chasing romance. Laugh, share, and experience life. We don't have time to throw our lives away! **We get one shot at life!**

CHAPTER SEVEN

Making Sense of Life

W hat does your life truly mean? Why do you even get up in the morning? Is your life significant? What really matters? What do you want out of life: to be attractive and wealthy, to be more popular, to have more sex, to plant a beautiful garden, to find a cure for a terrible disease? **What do you want?**

How do we determine if we are living meaningful lives?

I find that the two most significant actions that bring the most meaning into my life are: (1) serving others, and (2) striving to reach my potential. Of course, along the road of life I enjoy many things such as good music, good food, sharing with family and friends, traveling, sex, seeking spiritual fulfillment, and pondering the world and life. But if I were about to die and I were asked what has brought the most meaning into my life, I would say helping others and trying to be all that I am capable of being.

To be able to serve others and to better ourselves, we may need to improve our present situation and to become more self-reliant. If we are too down on ourselves, too into ourselves, or just simply lost in our own world, we will not be able to pursue these goals very well.

We have established three major ideas in this book: (1)

All of us are here for a reason, (2) We act according to the way we see ourselves, and (3) Our learned behaviors contribute significantly to why we are the way we are. So how can we use these three ideas to lead a more meaningful life?

Ask lots of questions. Why do some people seem so happy and others seem so miserable? Why do some people manage to stay out of trouble while others end up going to prison? Why are some people so down on themselves? Why are some people so confident? Why do some people think they are actually better than other people? Why are some people so mean and hateful? How do elderly people cope with life? **The beginning of living a more meaningful life is realizing that people are the way they are for certain reasons—they are not predestined to be that way.**

Our first concept is the idea that we are here for a reason. How would you feel if you actually believed that you are here for a reason as opposed to believing that you are just another being in a meaningless universe? Do you think you would look at yourself differently? Sure you would. Your life would have much more meaning because you would know in your heart that you have **true value.**

Now the idea that you are here for a reason infers that you were created by some kind of super intelligent being. Don't misunderstand me. This is not a religious book, but if the world has no creator, the only meaning that you and I are going to find is in the interactions that we have with all the other human animals on this earth. If there is no creator, there is no overall purpose for the world, no possible afterlife, and nothing greater than ourselves to have faith in. In other words, if there is no creator, this world is all there is. After we die, it's all over.

If we can bring ourselves to believe that we were created for a reason, our lives will take on tremendous significance. We will look forward to each day knowing that we have something to offer the world. We will know that we matter very much. We may even consider the idea that the creator is helping us through the trials of life.

The next concept is the idea that we act according to the way we see ourselves. The bottom line to this idea is that if we don't like the way we are or the way our lives are going, we need to learn to see ourselves differently.

My friend, one of the great secrets of life is understanding that there is so much more going on with people than we see on the surface. It's like seeing an attractive woman walk into a restaurant and some of the guys sneak a glance at her and try not to let their wives or girlfriends catch them. The guys are putting on a "front" to protect them from letting anybody know who they really are. Let's take a few other examples. Some attractive women walk around appearing to ignore people but it is obvious that they love the attention they are getting. Some macho guys walk around with a mean and tough look on their faces though they probably feel scared and weak inside, too. People who feel they are average act like they are average. People who are downcast or depressed practically ignore everyone and everything. They don't interact with the world very much because they just don't care.

To start seeing yourself differently, begin by being more real. If you lack confidence and are down on yourself, decide today to start living at least a little differently. Remember, it's your life at stake here. Start dressing better, walking taller, smiling more, being friendly, and interacting with people more.

The third concept is the idea that we have largely learned to act the way we do. **The way we act is the only way we know to act.** So we judge the world based on the way we see the world, and all of us see the world a little differently.

Just think--if you can change your behavior just a little, you will start **seeing yourself differently, so you will start** *acting* **differently**. The world will start responding to you in a more positive way. I guarantee it. Add to your thoughts the idea that you are here for a reason and you will be on the road to making sense of life!

Making Sense By Letting Life Teach Us

People who find real meaning in life possess another important quality: They are willing to let **all of life** teach them. They learn from the good and the bad, the wise and the foolish, the strong and the weak, the winners and the losers. These people understand that life exists to teach them, and that lessons can be found in practically every situation and experience. They understand that life is a sort of training ground that ultimately makes them what they become.

Some people see life through a narrowly focused lens. They think that life is good only for the winners, the wealthy, the beautiful, the scholarly, and the accomplished. They miss much because they do not see the beauty and complexity of life or how everything on earth and everything we experience makes us into the people that we become. The deepest meaning in our lives comes from the whole experience of our lives, not just selective experiences that we think are the secret of life.

Life is constantly giving us feedback. Life lets us know how we are doing. This very day we may stumble upon an idea or concept that excites us and totally turns our lives around. We may meet some person who knocks us off our feet. But we must be looking at life with the **expectation** that each day is going to offer us something new. If we see each day as a dull, mundane existence, we will miss much of what life is trying to show us.

Obviously, saying that life is trying to teach us something infers that there is a power, or force, or creator. An impersonal universe cannot "show" us anything. We can find comfort and meaning in the idea that the universe has logic and order. There is a scheme to life; life is not just some random happenings without meaning. There is a creator, and the maker of the universe is teaching us through all of the experiences of life.

You Have A Purpose For Being Here

One motivation for changing your life right now is that **you are here for a reason**. You make think that last statement is psychological mumbo-jumbo, but consider some things with me. What if the world was populated with all females or all males? What if there were no children or if people did not age at all? What if we all had equal capabilities so that we were not able to compete at sports, or to get a better job, or to excel at anything? How different would the world be?

The world has a scheme to it. It takes all of us to make to make our world exist. All of us are part of the whole. Do you see? The world is no accident; all of us matter very much. We may **feel** that we don't belong, but the feelings that we have are only learned feelings from past experiences. You and I are here for a reason, but we first must realize that the world is a logical place that makes sense. Otherwise, we may not be able to see our purpose or our value as humans.

Let's consider Joanna. Joanna was never able to see her value as a person. She was an average woman with average intelligence. He parents were low-keyed people who had average self-esteem, so Joanna had average self-esteem. She "got by" in life and tried not to ever rock the boat. Eventually Joanna met and married a great guy and the couple had four children. One child became a scientist who discovered a cure for a dreaded disease. Another child became a teacher who was one of the most popular teachers with her students for over 30 years. Still another child became a politician who brought about significant changes that helped millions of people. The last child became a comedian who made thousands of people laugh.

Do you think Joanna's life had purpose? She wasted a lot of her life thinking that her life did not have purpose because she did not have the insight to see that she, like all of us, has a purpose for being here. All of us add something to the world. If we feel that our lives do not have purpose, it is because we have lost our perspective on life. We may be too depressed, narrowly-focused, or selfish. We may be living in our own little world so much of the time that we don't really "get it" anymore. We may be missing out on living an exciting life because we have gotten off track and don't know how to get back on.

Right now, you and I have the chance to find more purpose in life. We are still here! **We are still alive! We have**

another day to live! We have the opportunity today to do something. Remember, it is not about what is going on around us or what we think about the future. **It is about what we are doing with what we have right now!**

Making Sense By Not Worrying So Much About What Others Think

Recently I visited a fifth grader who asked me to have lunch with him at school. As we sat together in the school cafeteria, I noticed that every time I said something to him, he glanced over at a couple of female classmates to get their reactions. He wanted me to be cool so I tried to be what I thought he wanted me to be. I was reminded once again how often many of us allow other people's thoughts to determine what we say and do. I understand that a lot of this is a natural part of growing up, but as adults can you see how this type thinking severely limits our own growth and creativity? If other people determine what we say and do, **who are we**? Aren't we allowing other people to run our lives? What would happen if we just tried to be ourselves? **Well, obviously we would act differently and people would respond to us differently.**

Worrying too much about what other people think will hold us back from being who we want to be. The sooner we realize that we need to be our own man or own woman, the sooner our lives will take on more significance. Think about the difference in the way I think and the way that fifth grader thinks. I really don't care what fifth graders think about me, but to him and his classmates it's almost a life and death situation whether or not their classmates like them.

Let's look at another example. David was in junior high. He felt that most people did not like him. Now, based on what we have said so far, why do you think that David felt that others did not like him? Well, his parents were not very sociable people. His mother had a drinking problem, so her negative thinking about life influenced David's thinking. David had also developed the habit of being a C student though he had the potential to do much better. He was not diligent enough in his studies or in his interactions with other people. He had learned not to be very sociable, so he became one of those students who are loners. Other people saw him as a loner. People avoided David because he avoided them. David began to see himself as a sort of rebel because he thought that being a rebel is what he was meant to be. Over time, his role began to feel right.

Eventually, David began to feel that he was the one who had it all together and that everyone else was messed up. So David spent the rest of his life acting out of the role that he had taken on in junior high. He often felt that his life lacked meaning and he often felt lonely, but he figured that's just the way life was. He missed a lot of opportunities to meet new people, to have more fun, and to have more meaningful experiences because he had locked himself into a lifestyle that he thought was the answer for him.

Many of us end up like David and we don't even realize it. We may decide that we were just meant to be a certain way. We may allow our families and friends to convince us that we are less than we really are. We may let other people do our thinking for us. We may allow ourselves to develop self-destructive ways of thinking and behaving. We may lose our hope and get to a point where we just really don't care what happens to us.

So why do we live? What is the point? What difference do our lives make? I believe that every life makes a difference in the world. I believe that all of us are part of a bigger picture that we do not fully understand.

Why do I write books? For one thing, I see so many disparities in life, and I am interested in why these disparities exist. Some people seem to have it all while others have very little. Some people seem to enjoy every day of life while for others life is a struggle to simply survive. I feel led to share my feelings and experiences, because my life experiences may be typical of what the average human being goes through.

I write books because I want other people to realize that life has been a struggle for me, too. Life is not easy. I have often wrestled with my own physical, emotional, and spiritual life. I can even remember as a young child wondering why some people were so hypocritical, and why certain people thought they were better than others, and why certain groups of people were down on other groups. And the people who were down on others saw themselves as being wonderful people! I have searched for the meaning of life for over 50 years.

All of us seem to have various reasons for living. Some of us want to be famous. Some of us live for our children. Some of us live just to survive. Some of us live for pleasure and some live for religion. Some of us just simply don't care.

My friend, **there must be more to the meaning of life than being attractive, accomplished, educated, popular and wealthy**. If there isn't, then much of the world is a pathetic mistake.

Let's consider that last thought. Without the masses of people, how would the attractive, accomplished, educated, popular and wealthy become what they are?

If we desire to live a more meaningful life, **we must see that it takes all of us to make the world go round.** What if there were only two people on the earth and one had more natural ability than the other? There is no way the more talented person could become educated to the degree that people are educated today. First, there would be no colleges. Next, there would not be a large body of knowledge to study because there would have been no other people to study the world. Also, what difference would it make how accomplished the person thought he was, because there would be only one person on earth (with less ability) to admire his abilities and accomplishments? What difference would it make how attractive the person was except possibly to the one other person? There would be no masses of people to look at him. Popularity would not be a major issue because there would only be one other person to be popular with.

The point of the preceding example is that we are part of the whole of humanity. We cannot live completely apart from society. **The world has to be the way that it is for us to be the way that we are.** If the world were not the way it is, our lives would be totally different. If there were not millions of people in the world, there would not be enough demand for the products of companies. There would be no economy. There would be no money for the government of a country to build roads, provide medical care, or to negotiate with other countries, and so on. Without large numbers of people, there would be no schools, concerts, congresses, policemen, firemen, sports teams, and so on.

Again, the point is that life makes sense. Because the world is the way it is, we are able to make money, have fun, find romance, enjoy people, discover new ideas, help others, learn about ourselves, and find meaning. And if we are dissatisfied with our lives, we have the potential to change. Our dissatisfaction with life will **drive** us towards the things we want and the way we want to be. Henry David Thoreau said, "The man who is not satisfied with his life, what can he not do?"

Many people who have already attained the so-called prizes of life (looks, education, accomplishments, popularity, wealth) take their lives for granted and do not even realize how fortunate they are. They don't even realize that it took the rest of the world to make them what they are. They think, "Well, this is just the way I'm supposed to be."

The point here is that **all of us matter very, very much!**

CHAPTER EIGHT

Making Sense
of the World

There is just so much about the world that we don't know. For example, scientists tell us how they believe the universe began and where people came from, but they have not quite figured out one tiny detail--the mechanism that made it all happen. While seeking to live a fulfilling life, it is helpful to realize that there is a lot going on that no one truly understands.

So far, we have discussed how to improve our self-concept and level of confidence and how to find more meaning in life. The next challenge that keeps us from throwing away our one shot at life is making some kind of sense of the world or putting the world in some kind of perspective. Just because we have confidence, good self-esteem, and meaning does not mean that the world will make any more *sense*.

Insights Into
Making Sense Of The World

One of the most important concepts in this book is the idea that we live in a fascinating world that gives us the opportunity to truly become whatever we want to be. We have a free will, so we can do whatever we want to do. However, just because we choose to go a certain direction, does not mean that the world will accept our point of view or that we will live the most worthwhile lives possible. The world has certain social and scientific laws that we cannot break without suffering the consequences. Some of us miss a lot of success in life by trying to bend these basic laws to suit our own desires.

There are two concepts that will help us understand the world. First, we are all meant to be different. We were not meant to be like everybody else. If we were all the same, we could not understand life on the level we do now. Second, all of us have been given the chance to become more than we are.

Many of the situations and people that we encounter in life are symbols that help us understand the world. (light, darkness, lion, lamb, day, night, girl, guy, rich, poor, good, evil, attractive, ugly).

For example, how many guys get to be the big movie star everyone admires and wants to be like? How many girls become the beautiful starlet that some girls wish they could be like? The answer to both questions is not very many. You see, if everyone were a movie star, there would be no movie stars, because being a star would be just an ordinary phenomenon. Why? Because there would be no audience. There would be little variation in the way people see each other. We would all be more or less alike.

Many of us feel that if we were movie stars then we would surely have found the secret of life. We would have lots of money. We would be admired by millions. Our faces would be shown all over the world. We could get any romantic interest we wanted. We would have power. We would have everything that we think that everyone wants.

The problem here is that being a movie star is not the secret of life. Many people find tremendous satisfaction and meaning in other aspects of life. People who strive to be like movie stars often forget the hard work that it takes to be an actor or actress. They forget about the extreme competition of continuing to get good roles. **And they forget that the reason we admire the movies so much anyway is because movies take us to places, dreams, and fantasies that most of us are not able to have in our everyday lives. If everyday life were like the movies, we would not need the movies.**

Movies help us to see ourselves more clearly and to understand ourselves better, because movies are *symbolic* of our dreams and fantasies. We see the tough, cool guy who always wins, never makes a mistake, and whom all the ladies want. We see the gorgeous woman who looks perfect and does everything right, and can have any guy. **In the movies, we see all that we wish we could be--and are not.**

Now, let's take this to the next level. All of life is life is this way. **We may be wasting a lot time and energy wishing we could be like someone else or be in another situation, but we become unable to see our own uniqueness.** We just know in our hearts that if we could be like certain other people that we would surely be happy. And we miss much of the purpose of *our* lives.

In reality, there are plenty of cool, attractive men and women who seem to have advantages over the rest of because coolness and good looks are valued highly in our society.

However, if people find meaning in their lives because they happen to have looks, money, or talent and this makes them feel better than others, these people are leading lack-luster lives. The meaning of life is not found by comparing ourselves to others or finding contentment by telling ourselves that we are better than everyone else. What kind of meaning would that be?

Likewise, people who feel that they are less than others because they lack money or because they do not have movie star looks, are also deceiving themselves.

The true meaning of life is elusive. If we cannot get past our **ego**, we may spend a lifetime searching for meaning that does not even exist. Finding meaning in life is a lifelong journey and it is a little different for each of us. **Only when we finally realize that we have the personal power to guide our own lives, only when we realize that each of us is very unique and precious in our own right, only when we are able to recognize the uniqueness of other people, only when we begin to believe in and value ourselves, only when we understand that everyone of us are in this thing together, only when we allow the power behind the universe to teach us what life is about........will we begin to find true meaning.**

All Of Us Can Become Great

All of us have the potential to become great. With diligence, commitment, and wisdom, we can accomplish more than we can imagine.

What is greatness? It is being a positive influence on our families, friends, and other people. It is giving our best effort in everything we do. It is being responsible and living the kind of lives that others will want to emulate. It is leaving the world a better place than the way we found it.

Becoming great involves **focusing on what we want to accomplish and having a strong sense that we are here for a reason. No one accidentally becomes great.** If we do not allow the trials, problems, and even the pleasures of this life to dominate our thinking, we can reach high levels of achievement. We need to focus on being the best we can be with our families and other people.

If we desire greatness, we will have to go after it. But if we are committed to being winners, life will reward us in surprising ways. Aim for success.

Making Sense Of The World
By Understanding That All Of Life
Is Open To Many Possibilities

The Trojan War was one of the most interesting events in history. (Archaeologists are finding evidence that the Trojan War really happened). In the story, Paris, the prince of Troy, abducts Helen, the wife of Menelaus, King of Sparta, and takes her to Troy and marries her. Menelaus is outraged when he hears that Paris has taken beautiful Helen away from him. Ultimately, these events lead to the Trojan War between Troy and Greece, partly because Menelaus wanted her back. Helen is known as the face that launched a thousand ships.

The Greeks often used the story of the Trojan War to help explain their understanding of human behavior. Will men go to war over a beautiful woman? How far will people go because of their passions? How much do people allow their feelings (and other people) to control their actions?

Just as the Trojan War was complex, **our lives are com-**

plex. Our lives could go in a thousand different directions because of our passions and desires if we could only realize that every day is abounding with possibilities. Excitement, adventure, and romance are in each of us if only we would let these feelings out.

Here is the point: **Each day our lives have the potential to go any number of directions**. Whenever we see a day as being ordinary or mundane, whenever we feel bored, whenever we think we already know the answers to the mysteries of life, we are only deceiving ourselves. Life is bigger than we are. Our passions are bigger than we are. We simply do not know how each day is going to turn out. We can make ourselves miserable by refusing to see life for what it is.

Take Natalie. Natalie was a gorgeous woman who turned heads everywhere she went. She could step into a restaurant and everyone in the restaurant would forget their reality for a moment and take time to look at Natalie. When this happened, everyone's passions were taking over. This was real life.

In Natalie's mind, she was more important than other people. It just made sense because of all the attention she got. Even other girls around Natalie felt less important because of the attention that Natalie received. Natalie lived in this bubble of hers thinking that she was living when realistically Natalie's life was more of a contrived game.

Of course, an attractive girl like Natalie had to have an attractive, cool guy. She had a reputation—it did not really matter so much what kind of person the guy was as long as he made Natalie look good so she could keep up the image she had of herself.

As far as some of the guys were concerned, they just

wanted to be around Natalie because she was a cute mass of flesh. Their deepest thoughts were not of what kind of personality she had, what kind of mother she would make, what kind of sense of humor she had or how much she cared for other people.

To live an honest life, it is helpful to focus on **who we** *really* **are rather than on who we think we are. Some psychologists call these different selves the real self and the false self. The false self always sabotages the real self because its motivations are short-sighted, habitual, contrived, learned, trivial, and ordinary. The false self thrives on the games people play.**

In case all of this is beginning to sound like psychological mumbo-jumbo, let's delve more deeply into these ideas. Remember, we are learning how to live the richest and most meaningful lives possible.

We often allow four or five people to determine how we see ourselves. These people may be close friends, family members, or co-workers. These people are around us so much that their opinions of us make us feel that we are really the way they think we are. Sometimes they make us feel good, other times not so good, because we live in their world. In other words, **we may not see the bigger world out there and the people that we could become.**

Consider Jill. Jill was an average girl who lived in a small town. She enjoyed life but she often felt that she was just passing time rather than pursuing her dreams. No one ever encouraged her to go after her dreams. She was just "here." When she woke up again, she would go through the same routine again, and this was Jill's life--very little excitement, passion, or hope.

Jill did not realize what she was missing and how much life was still in her until one of her basketball coaches convinced her that she was a special lady with tremendous potential. She became a basketball star in high school and college. She married a great guy and had two children. She also became a very successful business woman.

She went on to live a magnificent life. Her basketball coach made a tremendous difference in her life.

The Bottom Line To Finding Meaning

We live in interesting times but many of us are so caught up in the news, markets, entertainment, politics, and general happenings that we often fail to think about what we are really doing or what we are here for. Many of us are sleepwalking through life. In other words, a lot of us do little more than just respond to stimulus. To make matters worse, we respond in the way we have been conditioned to respond since we were five years old.

Many people feel that they are victims of life. These people feel that life is a struggle and there is not enough to go around. So they try to find security through money, status, accomplishment, or knowledge. They try to arrange the outside world so that they will feel safe, comfortable, and in control.

It does not dawn on them that making changes in themselves rather than trying to change the outside world is the answer.

If we do not want to throw away our one shot at life, we need to awaken to life. **To the degree that we realize that we** determine what happens to us is the degree to which we will experience meaning, fulfillment, and happiness. It is not what is going on around us that makes the difference......but what's going on within us.

So What Is The Answer?

The challenge of life is to accept ourselves as we are, with all our shortcomings, blemishes, and weaknesses, in a world that celebrates beauty, strength, accomplishment, self-indulgence, and self-sufficiency. The trick is to see our worth without allowing other people to make us feel less than we are.

We should stop trying to be somebody and--just be.

CHAPTER NINE

Becoming a Champion in the Game of Life

*E*very day, people die not having been able to say, "I made it," or "I heard people chanting my name," or "My life meant something."

Honestly, words are inadequate to express the supreme value that all of us have. One of the most beautiful lines I have ever heard expressing human value was in a song by the country group, The Statler Brothers. The song is dedicated to veterans who fought in the Vietnam War. The song captures the thoughts of a mother visiting her son's name on the Vietnam Wall in Washington, D.C. In one line, the mother says to the Lord, "Lord, will you tell him he's more than a name on a wall?"

It would be so wonderful if every person who comes into the world could realize his or her paramount value. So many times, before a child can even get a good grasp on life, the world begins to beat the child down. In a short time, the child loses faith in his abilities and begins to see what he **cannot** do. Life becomes drudgery rather than a miracle.

In this chapter, we are going to consider some ways that we can develop a winning edge so that we can become champions in life. Every one of us has the potential to be a champion.

Be A Champion By Being
Aware Of Our Amazing Freedom

It is almost frightening to think about how much freedom we have as humans to do whatever we want to do. If we want to kill ourselves, life will not stop us. If we want to act cool or silly, we can. If we want to hate ourselves, nothing is going to stop us. If we think we are better than other people, we are free to feel this way. If we think we are right about everything, no power is going to make us change. If we get our kicks by putting others down, we will have our reward right now. **We are free to think whatever we want to think, but we should understand that our thoughts and actions will have some consequences**. Again, we are connected to everyone else more than we may realize.

Realizing that our thoughts and actions have consequences can help motivate us to live more rewarding lives. Haven't you ever noticed someone doing something that was not in the person's best interest? Sure you have. All of us at one time or another make choices that are not in our best interest, but the problem is that we don't always have someone to tell us. For example, a guy may try to be overly cool in front of a woman who prefers guys who are more down to earth. Or someone may hurt his chances for getting a job or making a friend by using foul language in front of people who don't care for bad language.

One of the greatest revelations is that we have total freedom of thought, but this freedom of thought can be a blessing or a curse.

If we are not living fulfilling lives, we may want to examine some of our thoughts to see if we have lost our perspective. Remember, there are some basic realities in life no matter what we think. The main reality is that people want to be treated with respect and dignity.

Become A Champion By Overcoming Discouraging Feelings

When we feel down or depressed, we are more apt to let the world run over us and we are more likely to run over other people. We can come to be resentful. We may not be totally aware that we are doing this because our spirits are darkened by our trials, situations, and the opinion we have of ourselves. We can quickly get on shaky ground because we may get to a point where we don't care about anything.

We end up going to extremes. We treat some people with disrespect who we normally would treat with kindness. Our thoughts, opinions, and actions may become skewed or influenced by our depressed attitude. We may end up hurting ourselves, others, and our chance for happiness. When we come out of it, if we come out of it, we don't understand why some people look at us with suspicion.

The human mind is extremely complicated. **Every person I know gets in moods and they do not even realize when they are "in" a mood.** Think about the many directions from which people come. Some people are very religious and some people hate the idea of God or any kind of religion. Some people feel that they are right about everything and others feel that they know very little about anything. Some people live for sex and pleasure, some live to serve others, and some people just don't care.

If we do not want to throw away our one shot at life, it

is very important to understand how imperfect other people are. It is important to understand that many people operate largely out of self-interest. Seldom will people deny their own well-being for the compassionate feelings they have for others.

Please don't misunderstand me--I very much realize that there are plenty of heroes and heroines in the world. But I am speaking more about the average daily interactions that we have with people. We do not want to be naive.

All of us are imperfect. We see what we want to see, and we act more out of our perceptions and passions than we do logic and facts. This being the case, we will find more meaning in life by realizing that when we feel down, depressed, or not with it, we are probably being unfair to ourselves by letting our possibly distorted perceptions of ourselves and others color the way we see life.

The bottom line is that the world is so complicated that our meaning and happiness is something that we largely create from within.

Be A Champion By
Maintaining A Winning Attitude

I find that we do better in life when we keep ourselves up, that is, feeling good about ourselves and feeling some-what in control. If we are not careful, we will let ourselves slip into a mental state that hurts us more than we realize. We are not necessarily aware when this happens. **Being aware of how our attitude affects our outside world can help us not throw away our one shot at life.** Let's take a closer look at what I am saying.

When I began to really enjoy life about 20 years ago, a number of positive situations and experiences happened in my life. I stopped drinking alcohol and smoking pot. I met a nice woman who came from a positive, well-adjusted family. I started taking some risks such as public speaking. I went back to school and got a college degree. In general, I felt much better about myself so **I began to view all of life more favorably.**

As I learned to see life from a more favorable point of view, I felt better about myself and more in control of my life. Reality became more pleasant. I had less of a need for alcohol, drugs, or anything that would make me want to escape from life because **I did not need to escape from life.**

Over time, whether we are generally happy or generally down, situations can come into our lives that can begin to erode our mental health. It can be a problem in a relationship. It can be a mistake or a poor choice. (We are human.). It can be the loss of a job or our health. It can be the loss of loved ones. It could be that we lose our perspective and base our lives too much on pride or some other false prop. Whatever the case, we begin to go downhill emotionally.

We may become more susceptible to becoming depressed. We may be more apt to abuse alcohol and drugs. We may slowly get to a point where we don't care much about anything. **At this dangerous point, we may be headed down**. I have seen it happen to me again in my later years. I have had to work very hard to regain emotional health.

It is critically important for us to understand that the life we are living right this minute, that is, the present emotional state that we are in, is not the only possible one for us. **We are going to go up or down based on the degree of dili-**

gence that we put into protecting our present emotional state and the way we respond to the unforeseen situations that are going to come our way. If we are up right now, we need to work at staying up. If we are down, we need to take some actions that will help us feel better about ourselves.

Few of us will admit it, but all of us come to a point in our lives where we feel helpless. Why? Because we have not been beyond our present level of emotional maturity and understanding. **At this point, either we have to change somehow and go to the next level of maturity, or do nothing and accept ourselves as we are with the same shortcomings, resentments, and drawbacks that have held us back.** Instead of truly living and creating new possibilities for ourselves and the other people in our lives, we end up playing the same old roles over and over because we will not let ourselves go to the next level. We play the role of the "pretty girl who everybody likes and envies," or the "star athlete," or the "unlucky one who is meant to lose," or "the one who is always in control because he has all the money," or "the one who blames everyone and everything in the universe because he or she cannot be happy," or "the one who feels that life owes him or her," or "the martyr who helps a lot of people but often feels resentful." Our role is what we become and it is the role we die in if we do not reach for the next level. Instead of living, we end up playing a role and we cannot understand why we are not happy.

Consider Linda. Linda was an average girl throughout high school, but during her junior year she turned into a super athlete. She became more shapely and eventually she met a guy whom she was crazy about. Her basketball and track teams were very successful largely because of Linda's talent. Linda was cheered on at every sports event and she was frequently written up in the papers. Linda was on top of the world.

When Linda went to college she had grown accustomed to getting a lot of attention. But no one at college knew Linda, so she did not get the kind of attention she thought she deserved. This made her feel depressed which showed up in her athletic endeavors and in her overall attitude. Linda was not able to reach her greatest capacities because she did not fully realize that she still had to give her best to life everyday.

Life never becomes automatic. To get and keep a winning edge demands that we soar like eagles everyday.

QUESTIONS TO PONDER

- What are some of the advantages and disadvantages of having a free will?

- If we stay down or depressed a lot, can we expect to be true champions in life?

CHAPTER TEN

Ways to Get a Winning Edge

realistically, the world is so complex and beyond our understanding that our minds cannot comprehend **true reality**. All of us operate out of our own sense of how we see life and the world, and our perception really bears little resemblance to the real world. There are so many religions, cultures, opinions, and daily happenings that it would be impossible for our minds to understand it all. So we create our own little way of looking at the world so that we can function. This being the case, it behooves us to create the most pleasant reality in our minds that we can.

Though it may sound ridiculous, we should choose to be happy and successful whether it makes sense or not. We will never find the exact circumstances that will give us a winning edge constantly. What happens to us is determined by what we focus our thoughts on the most and how diligently we pursue our dreams.

Develop An Edge
By Hanging In There

How many come-from-behind victories have you seen in your life? What kinds of players manage to come from behind when the game seems hopeless? They are the players who stay focused on the game and **never give up. They are the players who have developed a winning edge.**

Sometimes, if we can just hang in there a little longer, we can buy some time that may help us to win later. I talk a lot in this book about changing, but **it's not always a matter of changing; sometimes it is simply a matter of hanging in there right now.** Stop and consider the consequences. How many decisions have you made that you would like to have the opportunity to try again?

Developing a winning edge is a matter of our winning some battles by making the decision to hang in there no matter what happens.

Develop A Winning Edge By Being
Sure You Are On The Right Track

Many people pursue activities and possessions that they think will make them happy. They may have a beautiful home, a nice car, a successful career, or the sought- after mate. Often these people are still miserable. They not only have taken the wrong track, they don't even know where the track is.

True happiness comes from within. We are happy because we exist, because we have the chance to live another day to do better, and to develop our potential.

To develop a winning edge, we need to be sure that we

are on the right track. How can we get somewhere if we don't know where we are going? Focus on success.

Gain An Edge By Putting Yourself In The Place Of Other People

If you were the child of a president or a king, is it possible that you might see life just a little differently? What if you had been born to parents who were poor and uneducated? Do you think that event might color the way you look at life? It's obvious that all of us see life differently. The challenge is to recognize our differences and to interact with other people in a way that benefits all of us.

Understanding why people behave the way they do will give us an edge. Most human behaviors can be traced back to the beginning of the human race.

Some great teachers throughout history have taught us that the generations who went before us--all the way back to beginning of civilization--had a tremendous influence on the way we behave. For example, some of us are great hunters and fishermen because our ancestors were great hunters and fishermen. Some of us are superb athletes or warriors for the same reason. Some of us have a lot of charisma because we inherited some of the feelings and energy from people who have gone before us.

It is apparent that negative feelings and energy are also passed on through the generations. Many families have almost constant trouble and turmoil because of the negative behaviors and feelings that are passed from one family to the next. It is no secret that suicide often runs in families. Usually, the only way to change this situation is for a family

107

member to become aware of the situation and to personally change creating more positive feelings and behaviors for the family. **The people who make these changes actually alter history.** They create a much better environment for their families right now and for the generations to come.

If we are aiming for success, it is crucial to understand why other people are the way they are. Winners have empathy for other people. Winners are willing to help others because they understand that there are reasons why people behave the way they do.

Get A Winning Edge
By Encouraging Others

Tempers were flaring and emotions were raging in the small southern high school. The boys and girls in the Gatlin family were tired of being put down. They had finally been pushed to their limit like wildcats trapped in a corner.

There were two girls and two boys in the Gatlin family. They were not very well off and they could not afford to wear clothes as nice as the "cool" crowd. The Gatlins were down on themselves largely because other kids at school put them down and made fun of them.

The cool crowd spent a lot of time keeping the Gatlins "in their place." They wanted to keep the Gatlins in a box. They would not give the Gatlin kids a chance to do better. They were going to make sure that the Gatlins never thought more highly of themselves.

But on this day, the Gatlins had had enough. Big John Gatlin knocked Huey Camden over two tables and into the wall, while Jimmy Gatlin hit Rickey Johnson six times in the face before Rickey could even get his fists up. The Gatlin girls, Judy and her sister Jolene, were holding their own, too. They slung Kaila and Alethea, the two most popular girls in school, into a big smelly garbage can. There was almost a riot until the principal broke it up.

The cool crowd was definitely in the wrong. They wanted to make sure that as few people as possible were ever threats to their position as the most popular and admired kids in school. They did not want other people to do better. This was their show and the rest of the world had better get out of their way. But they failed to understand that most people can only be pushed so far.

Even though on this day the Gatlins stood up for themselves and came out on top, this story does not have a happy ending. Over the years, the cool crowd had done their job well. None of the Gatlins were able to overcome the negative feelings caused by all the ridicule they had received.

John and Jimmy Gatlin both lived the better part of their lives with low self-esteem. Both had average jobs. Judy Gatlin was married twice but could not seem to adjust very well to marriage. Jolene killed herself when she was 22.

Huey, Rickey, Kaila, and Alethea all went on to college and became "successful" as far as the prizes of this world are concerned. However, all of them lived basically shallow and confused lives and none of them did very much to encourage others or to help the world be a better place.

What could the so-called cool crowd have done to help themselves and others feel better? They could have developed a winning edge by encouraging others.

When we encourage others, everybody wins. When we put others down, everybody loses, including ourselves.

Get The Edge By
Realizing Why We Are Here

All of us are here to bring good to the world. Once we become aware of our gifts, talents, and passions, we should use them and share them with others. **Helping ourselves and others brings great meaning into our lives.** We are here to use our God-given abilities to help and serve others.

Please do not make the mistake of feeling that you have no gifts, talents, or passions. **All of us have something to give.** You may not be able to see your value yet, but don't give up. If you feel you don't have anything to give, you are holding yourself back.

There is hope for you. Things are going to start changing for you. You have tremendous potential to be happy. I want to inspire you reach for the stars and to start living a life that you can feel good about. My friend, give life your best shot! There is no one in the universe just like you. Wake up to the possibilities in your life. **Never, never give up!**

Get The Edge By
Deciding To Interact With Life

The score was tied 7 to 7 in the regional football playoffs. Overton High School had the ball on their own 40-yard line with time enough to run one play. Johnny Randolph knew that his team would be running a pass play and he would be the receiver. After all, Johnny was one of the reasons Overton was in the playoffs. Johnny had worked hard all season to be the best receiver he could be and now the whole season came down to this one play.

As Johnny lined up for the play, he began to feel unsure of himself. "What if I miss the ball? Everyone will always blame me for losing the championship. What if I slip and fall down? What if the ball hits me right in the hands and I drop it?" Suddenly Johnny began to realize that he was hurting his own chances for making the play have any possibility of working out. He began to have more confident thoughts. He told himself, "I can do this. I am one of the reasons we are here to begin with."

Johnny felt a surge of power come over him. When the ball was snapped, he lit out like a demon. The quarterback threw a beautiful 60-yard pass and Johnny jumped high in the air at the one-yard line and caught the pass for the winning touchdown. Johnny was the hero of the game.

In the game of life, everyday is our championship game. All of us face doubts and we wonder if we have the ability to make the winning play. Like Johnny, we may play the "what if" game. We may hold ourselves back from all kinds of enjoyments by constantly doubting ourselves. What if she says no when I ask her out? What if I look stupid when I audition for the cheerleading squad? What if I can't do well in college? What if I can't play that musical instrument? What if people don't like me? What if I drop the ball in the championship game? What if, what if, what if! We turn into a person who doubts himself. Our doubt even shows on our faces.

If we do not want to throw away our one chance at life, we need to focus on being more confident. If we allow the "what if" side of ourselves to win all the time, we are going to lose a lot of "championships." When we at least try to be more self-assured, life will start being more fun. If we allow the doubtful side of ourselves to rule us, we end up creating our own misery. If there is one major idea I want you to understand in this book, it is: **You and I are creating our lives from moment to moment. The way we see ourselves right now is determining what is happening to us.**

If we see men or women who appeal to us and we are too shy to strike up a conversation, we will be people who are too shy to start up a conversation. If we decide not to participate in any kind of sports or activities, we will be people who do not participate in sports or activities. If we do not study hard in school, we will be people who make poor grades. If we are constantly down on ourselves, we will be people who feel inadequate.

In a sense, it really does not matter how we rationalize the way we are. We may feel that we are loners, or that we are shy, or that we don't like to get involved, but the truth is we are still going to suffer the consequences of our behavior. We may end up staying at home and wishing we could be with a certain man or woman. **We may wish that we could be an athlete or musician or writer, but unless we're doing something to make it happen, we will live in a world of make believe and fantasy.** If we are down on ourselves, we are pushing people away from us. If we are holding ourselves back in any way, we are selling ourselves short. The longer we hold ourselves back, the more of a habit it becomes. **The years slowly pass by and we end up living average lives and wishing that things could have been different.**

We Can Find Contentment

Contentment comes from living well and making wise choices. **Happiness is a result, not a possession.** It is the natural result of living a well-balanced life that is rewarding and satisfying.

Life is an opportunity. Each day we have another chance to do better. We are given a relatively short time in the overall scope of eternity to make the most of ourselves.

Life is a constant **learning experience**. If we are not happy, there are reasons for our discontentment. We should strive daily to reach for higher levels of life satisfaction. **It is possible to live more exciting, abundant lives.** I know this is true because I spent a large part of my life feeling discouraged and hopeless. But ultimately I decided to take charge of my life and make some major changes.

We should let life teach us. Be willing to make some changes. Have the courage to face yourself. Decide once and for all that you are going to take careful aim at success and find some real contentment.

Develop A Winning Edge By Truly Giving Value To Others— A Memorial To Tracy Renee Owen

Tracy Renee Owen was a lovely, 32-year old woman who had a great attitude. She was always smiling. She was a vivacious bighearted young lady who loved everybody. She was due to give birth any day when her life ended abruptly.

Tracy was shot to death in Nashville, Tennessee on January 5, 2004. She was out walking early that morning and stumbled and fell down. As she lay helpless on the ground, two men came by in a pickup truck. They stopped and while Tracy was crying for help, one of the men shot her five times in the upper body. She may have been in labor when she was killed. I can just see Tracy's yearning eyes saying, "please don't kill me."

I want to make Tracy's precious life mean even more for generations to come by writing about her in this book. I feel close to Tracy though I never met her. Her senseless death touched me and opened up a wellspring of emotions that I have not felt in a long time. Her life had a profound meaning for me in her death, and I know that she touched many lives in her day to day living.

Through Tracy, I am reminded of how utterly precious every human being is. I think about her child who never had a chance to live. I think of how often we hear of similar incidents and maybe we are stunned and sorrowful for a few minutes, but before long our minds are back at our routines.

Perhaps we are rushing through life thinking that happiness is "out there" somewhere. Maybe we are not slowing down long enough to appreciate our precious fellow human beings. Perhaps we are searching for some kind of meaning and we do not realize that **life is right before our eyes and it is called love. Maybe, we do not realize how precious each of us are. All of us are affecting other people whether we realize it or not.**

Even though I discuss changing and making wise decisions in this book, the real beginning for anyone who really wants to live a deep, rich, meaningful life is feeling true compassion for humankind. **Human beings are so precious. Tracy and her child were so precious.**

If I have said nothing so far to persuade you start living a more meaningful life, maybe you will get a spark of desire to live a more rewarding life because of Tracy. Maybe you are on the verge of hurting someone. Maybe you hate life and everybody. Maybe you just don't care about anything. Maybe you have plenty of material possessions but no true meaning in your life. If you choose to make some significant changes in your life based on something I have said about Tracy, you will be one of the many people that Tracy is going to influence for years to come

Tracy's live meant something. The life of her unborn child meant something. Your life......means something.

Get The Winning Edge
By Realizing That We Have Power

Today is our day and our time. We may feel down at the moment, but consider how our feelings change. We don't usually feel down all the time. The problem is that when we are in a low mood, we may miss opportunities that come our way. It is better to try hard to feel better because when we stay down too long, **we are only hurting ourselves**. To be happy, we should try to overcome some of our negative feelings or we are going to miss thousands of good times.

The best way to overcome our negative feelings is to concentrate on our strengths. It is very hard to totally overcome our weaknesses. If we can build on our strengths, we will have a much better chance to be happy.

All of us have personal power. This power helps us through life even when life is difficult. Our personal power gives us the strength to handle whatever life throws at us. It is important to understand that we still have personal power even though our lives may not be going well. This is the point where many people fail to take charge of their lives. They feel hopeless and out of control and they convince themselves that they have no power and that life itself is controlling them. **When we feel hopeless, we act like there is no hope and we sometimes sabotage our own chances for success.**

No one is totally happy all the time. All of us get sick, face daily challenges, and eventually die. But even though life can be extremely difficult for many of us, our painful memories can motivate us and be a great source of wisdom.

If we can begin to realize that we do have personal power, it is possible to start living lives that will be more meaningful and rewarding.

What if you decided that you were going to play the role of a winner rather than that of a loser? Wouldn't you have a positive influence on your family, friends, and other people? What if you decided that you were really smart and cool and that people who don't spend time with you are really missing out on something good?

What if you came to believe that you have personal power? How might your life change? My friend, this is your life. **Make it count. Feel your power.**

Seek Wisdom And Understanding

Very few people seem to actually be searching for true meaning in life. Few people seem to be seeking **wisdom and understanding** which are the **real treasures** of life. Few people seem to have any real substance.

I see people trying to buy happiness when all the great books of wisdom tell us that happiness can't be bought. I see people concentrating on their health but not their spirituality. People want to be healthy but they really don't know why.

They seem to feel that this is it so they soak up the pleasures of the world like a sponge.

Few people seem to stand for anything anymore. Few people seem to inspire real hope in other people. The main goal of many people is to help themselves and not serve their fellow humans and contribute something to the welfare of the human race.

Why Does The World Seem So Strange Sometimes?

Sometimes the world may seem insane. This is because there are so many people with so many different ways of looking at life. Most people see life through some kind of lens such as religion, science, wealth, security, or power. These symbols are what help us to relate to others. For example, people who consider morals and submission to higher authority to be important tend to lean toward religious ways of thinking. People who see the world from a cause and effect point of view tend to lean toward science.

The problem is that many people think that their point of view is the only possible way for things to be. So rather than trying to work with others, they spend a lot of time trying to convince others that they are right. These people do not find the deepest meaning in life because they do not realize that **all of life is important. Life exists to teach us something about ourselves.**

What Is The Bottom Line
To Developing A Winning Edge?

One of the secrets to the mysteries of life is realizing **there is more to life than we realize.** Life is more than being religious. It is more than being the coolest or most popular. It is more than sex. Life is more than just raising kids. It is more than our particular point of view.

Life is actually a collection of feelings, desires, lusts, dreams, doubts, pains, joys, needs, wants, aspirations, and disappointments. Every moment, we are sizing up our life in relation to everyone else. **But this moment is our life** and life is never perfect.

All of us are human. All of us have hopes and fears. All of us have fantasies, habits, loves, and hatreds. But we hold ourselves back in many ways. We limit what we are able to accomplish because of our fear of failure or feelings of inadequacy. We feel that if we can't be the very best, we won't be anything. Whether we are writing a book, writing a song, or becoming a star athlete, we allow the world to hold us down because of our perceived shortcomings. Many of us fail to give the world the gift of our talent, knowledge, wisdom, and compassion.

The Madness And Sadness Of It All

I am especially in touch with the difficulties that many people experience because I work in a hospital and I visit prisons every week.

Many times when I go to the prisons, the inmates and I discuss what life is really all about. They pour out their souls.

In many cases, the inmates need a cleansing of their feelings and emotions. Their family and friends are down on them. They have totally lost their direction and have very little hope about the future. They feel trapped in life, and they have gotten so down that they don't even know where up is. They need encouragement more than the flowers need the rain. They need a spark of hope.

All of us need hope because hope is the lifeline to tomorrow. But there is certain madness to life that makes it difficult for us. If we could just learn to look beyond ordinary life and see ourselves and the world in a different way, we would have a much better chance to be successful as humans.

Unfortunately, we have a tendency to see ourselves and other people as winners or losers, cool or not cool, attractive or unattractive, lucky or unlucky. We feel we either have it or we don't. Those who feel they have it also feel that they deserve all the rewards of life, and those who feel they don't have it feel that they deserve very little. They feel that they are just a mistake in a strange world that is hard to understand. So many people go through life playing the games that people play and living on memories.

Life Does Not Seem To Be Fair

There is no doubt that on the surface of things, life does not seem fair. Is it really fair that one woman is so attractive that all the guys want to date her while some other women would be happy if just one guy called them? Is it fair that some people have athletic abilities that cause them to be admired and other people can hardly walk? Is it fair for bullies to push weak people around just because they can? Is it fair that some people are born into wealth and others into poverty? Is it fair that some people have cancer and die young? Is it fair that God does not do away with all the injustices of the world with one mighty sweep?

How do we make sense of it all? Do we just accept life as it is? Do we just assume that life is just the way it is and that there is nothing we can do about it? Do we just assume that we are the way we are and there is nothing we can do to help ourselves?

Can we see the hopelessness in having an attitude of self-pity?

What Do We Want Out Of Life?

It is helpful to consider what we want out of life. Many people never take an honest look at what they really want. They may desire lots of things like money, women, men, popularity, artistic talent, athletic ability, a successful career, or love. In the end, though, they often have a hazy, unclear idea about what would really make them happy.

I am convinced that the most important need of every person is to feel important and valuable. People need to feel that they matter, but it is not easy to feel wanted and needed. As we have discussed, the world is not fair. There are disparities in people's incomes, physical looks, physical abilities, and mental abilities. **To find some true happiness in this life, we have to come to some kind of understanding about ourselves and our true role in the universe.** How can we do this?

Happiness is not found in any one thing. Happiness is a collection of feelings and emotions. Let's consider this idea while we consider how we learned to be the way we are. The following exercise is to help us see how our surroundings have impacted the way we feel about ourselves.

Pretend for a moment that you are suspended in space and there is nothing around you. All you can see is the color blue. Right now, there is nothing to make you feel particularly good or bad. How do you feel at the moment? Probably rather strange, since there are no scenes, people, or situations to see or relate to. Keep in mind there is no time, no future or past. There is nothing, no money, food, houses, schools, churches, or government. There are no family members, no friends, no jerks. There is no music, sex or athletics.

Now let's start adding factors to your world. Picture your parents in the scene with you. Your parents were complicated people. They may have been encouraging or discouraging parents. They may have been too strict, didn't want you around very much, or they may have loved the ground you walked on. Whatever the case, they had a lot to do with how you learned to see the world.

Next, add the house you grew up in. Was it an attractive house, an average house, or a below average house? How did you feel about the house? Did you feel ashamed of your house or did you feel proud? Add your feelings about your house to your scene.

Add some teachers to your scene. Were they encouraging, compassionate, understanding teachers? Did they tend to favor those who made better grades and had better behaviors? Were they always fair? How did your teachers make you feel?

Now add some people around the neighborhood and school. Maybe some of the people were really nice people.

Were there any bullies? Were there any people who put you down and called you names? Were there any people who thought they were better than you?

You get the idea. You and I started out as basically good and worthwhile people, but all the people and situations that came into our lives began to shape the way we looked at life. We learned to feel good or bad about ourselves. The world molded us into what we are today. **Our attitudes were largely determined by the world we grew up in.**

It is important to understand why we are the way we are so that we can see more clearly that we can create a new life for ourselves. We do not have to continue being the way we are. When we begin to understand ourselves, we can begin to see life differently.

The Greatest Danger In The World

Earlier in this book, I discussed the eight great dangers of the world. Now, I want to discuss the greatest danger that we face. **The greatest danger we face is going through life being unaware of ourselves and what we may be missing.**

Life is very dangerous and all of us are very vulnerable. I can share ideas and concepts with you, but ultimately the wisdom you attain will come through your own experiences. The information here is a guide to help you make as few mistakes as possible. My friend, if you are unfulfilled, there are reasons you feel the way you do.

Becoming More Positive Is A Great Start Toward Developing A Winning Edge

Scientists are beginning to understand that negative thinking actually hurts the body and positive thoughts heal the body. Having positive thoughts soothes our minds and helps our bodies function more properly. Positive emotions actually help our mental focus. Consider all the studies that have been done on the terminally ill and how that being positive helps them live longer. If being more positive can actually help us mentally and physically, we should make being more positive a major goal.

What does being more positive really mean? We tend to think that it means that we should constantly think positive thoughts. Trying to think positive thoughts all the time is unrealistic. All of us face trials in life. Being more positive actually means that we have more strength and courage to handle whatever life throws at us. Being positive is developing an attitude that helps us to see life as an experience between **us and life** rather than seeing life as an experience between us and others' expectations and opinions of us.

All of us have different experiences in life. If we spend our lives trying to be someone else, we are going to experience a lot of frustration and disappointment. **We are who we are.** Some of us have tremendous talents and abilities. Some of us have to face sickness, depression, poverty, and the death of loved ones. Some of us go to war. Some of us have hangups that are very difficult to overcome. **The point is that if we are going to live a rewarding life, we need to learn to play the cards we were dealt.** No matter how we see life at this moment, believe me, things are going to change drastically as time goes by.

It is important for us not to overvalue ourselves, that is, to feel that somehow we are the chosen few to receive life's rewards. To a degree, all of us have a grandiose opinion of ourselves, even more than we may realize. On the other hand, it is just as important not to feel that we are the unfortunate, unlucky few that destiny has frowned on. This type of thinking is one reason the world has the problems that it has.

We experience life on different emotional levels. We should focus on seeing life more realistically. For example, I am over 50 years old and I am not particularly appealing to young women--even if appealing to them were the fondest dream of my life. But if I fight life, I am really just fighting my own feelings. I may be envious of people who are extremely attractive, wealthy or talented because it seems that they are having most of the fun. But feeling sorry for myself and living in self-pity only hurts me and those around me. Besides, the truth is they are not having all the fun.

Being positive is being able to accept ourselves as we are. As a young man, I often thought that if I could be with certain girls, that my life would be heaven on earth. But, girls are also human. They, too, often go after the coolest and best looking guys. I spent a lot of time being depressed because I realized that most girls were not going to sacrifice what they wanted (or what they thought they wanted) just to make me feel better. **Basically, I was not accepting myself or life in a realistic way.**

Let's take this deeper. We are trying to see ourselves in a more realistic way. It is not possible for life to be fun all the time. All of us spend a lot of time with ourselves. **If we want to accomplish anything in this life, we have to push on. We have to overcome whatever thoughts and obstacles are holding us back. We have to develop a winning edge.**

I can see myself as an unattractive loser and a pathetic mistake in this life with nothing to offer the world. Or I can see myself as a wise, worthwhile, and encouraging person who has a purpose for being here on Earth. I don't have to tell you which view of myself is going to cause me to live a more meaningful, rewarding, and satisfying life.

QUESTIONS TO PONDER

- Does having a winning edge come from having favorable circumstances or the attitude that we have within us?

- How can we know that we are going in the right direction in our lives?

- What is the most important need of every person in the world?

- What is the greatest emotional danger in the world?

- How does the way we see ourselves affect the kind of lives we live?

CHAPTER ELEVEN

Secrets of Success

*L*et's consider an average day in our lives. All of us get up and have general routines. We probably check out the news of the day or at least overhear some news while we are getting ready. We make sure our family is ok and we prepare for the day. We then go out and live out our day. It's just another day.

Is this day any more important than any other day? Was this day 100 years ago anymore important than today? To the people who lived 100 years ago, that day was important. They had their own problems, challenges, desires, and wants. The same will be true 100 years from today.

The point is that life goes on and history unfolds. We could have lived in 1508, 1808, 1908, or 2008. **This day is not what is important—we are important. Our attitude, our self-image, and our degree of courage are going to determine what happens to us today. It's not what the day brings to us, but what we bring to the day.** There was news and happenings in 1898 and there will be the same in 2408. **It is what you and I are doing with this day that matters.**

Reawaken The
Possibilities In Your Life

When we feel that we have few choices in life, we put ourselves in a self-imposed prison. Having choices is real freedom. Think about it. If we have felt for a long time that there is nothing we can do to make our lives better, we have given ourselves a life sentence in a mental prison.

Having choices is necessary if we are going to have good mental health. The truth is that all of us have many possibilities, but we may have lost sight of them for various reasons. **Having possibilities is the essence of human existence.** If we feel hopeless and helpless, we are not going to be as happy as we could be.

Consider Lucy's story. Lucy West had failed at life many times. It seemed that everything Lucy had ever tried to do did not work out. She would meet a nice guy and he would turn out to be a frog. She would meet new friends, draw close to them, and then they would take advantage of her. She would come close to getting a really good job and someone else would swoop it out from under her.

Over the years, Lucy began to feel boxed in by life. She felt that it did not matter what she did, because nothing would work out anyway. Lucy got to a point where she felt that she did not have many choices. She felt trapped by life.

Eventually, through taking a hard look at her life, Lucy began to realize that her feelings of helplessness and hopelessness were keeping her from being happy. Lucy needed to learn that there were still plenty of possibilities in life, but that it was up to her to discover them. She needed to expand her way of looking at life because she had learned to feel helpless and to have a cynical attitude toward life. Lucy learned to feel in control of herself and she became a very happy, influential young lady.

Live With Passion

Every day is another opportunity to make something happen in our life. The sad thing is that we don't always live with passion. There is so much more life and spirit in us than we realize, but often we don't have the right situations or people to bring out our passion.

Think about the last time a movie made you want to cheer or cry. Think about a special occasion that brought your deepest emotions out. You know in your heart that you are really passionate about life.

We do not take advantage of every day that we are given. We may stay so wrapped up in the general business of life that we forget to live. We forget to dream. We forget how extraordinary all of us are and forget the tremendous potential that every one of us has.

Still, we have to believe in our hearts that life is a marvelous experience. Are we giving life our best shot or do we have a defeated attitude? Are we going the extra mile to make life more exciting for ourselves, our families, our friends, and others?

Find success by living passionately.

Getting Back On Track
By Planning Our Lives Daily

Life becomes more exciting when we live daily with some kind of plan in mind. To make a plan, we should ask ourselves some questions. What do we want to accomplish in life? How do we want to be remembered? What do we want to do for our children?

When Saturday morning rolls around at my house, my family and I gather together for a few minutes to relax and to decide what we want to do with the day. **We realize that what we do with each day is going to determine the kind of overall life that we live**. No day is ordinary. Each day matters. No day "just happens."

Let me share some of my goals with you. This is my second book. My next goal is to write a book with my teenage son. I believe this project would be special for him and for me. When I am no longer living, he will always have "our" book to reflect on and the memories of writing the book with me. I also want to write a song with him. I also want to share the deepest love possible with my wife.

It is helpful to remember that life here on Earth does not last forever. This may not be a pleasant thought, but it's just the way things are.

It is also helpful to search for balance in our lives. For example, I write books but I also want to get better at Taekwondo. I want to spend some time helping children, other adults, and prison inmates believe in themselves. I want to enjoy the uniqueness of other people. I want to have better health and to be spiritually stronger. All of these goals take effort and diligence on my part *daily*. **I simply cannot** wait for some golden tomorrow to magically make my dreams come true. *This* moment is life.

The Deceitfulness Of Prosperity

One of the great dangers of living in prosperous times is failing to live life with any sense of urgency. It is so easy to have pleasurable days, yet not realize that life is slowly getting away from us. If we have goals, we have got to focus on disciplining ourselves to see that daily life is not just some mysterious phenomenon in which we seek to grab all the fun we can, but a marvelous and fascinating experience that is teaching us about ourselves. The environment around us is the stage that our creator placed us on. When life is too easy, we may not have any reason to see aspects of our lives that could bring great meaning to us. **We may actually believe that we are really happy without realizing what we are missing.**

Every day we see people rushing through life. Many people seem to be letting the external events of their lives rule their days rather than trying to live in the present moment with all the excitement each moment offers. If we are not awake to life, we may have no idea what is really going on.

Consider Lynn's life. Lynn was happy with her life. She and her husband had good friends and they usually spent time with them on the weekends. They were well off financially so they were able to partake of the good things in life. However, as the years passed, Lynn began to feel empty. She began to see shortcomings in her children that she felt she could have changed had she been more **aware of the moments of her life.** She began to see certain improvements

131

in society that she could have been instrumental in changing or influencing if she had not been so adamant in thinking that she knew all the answers to life and that she and her friends had found "it." She began to feel that in some ways she had missed out on the true *meaning* of life.

The point here is not that Lynn had a bad life. Lynn lived a very enjoyable life. It's just that Lynn could have lived a much more rewarding life than she did if she had spent some time reflecting on the meaning of her life. But now, it is too late to start over. Lynn is sick and has only a few months to live.

Everything Has Its Time

If we are not aware of time and our own immortality, we may miss great opportunities in our lives. Recently, I watched the fourth installment of the Rocky movies starring Sylvester Stallone. I was reminded the movies demanded that Mr. Stallone be in top physical shape. Stallone could not wait until everything was right to make these movies. He was aware of time and he knew that he was not getting any younger. If he waited too long, he might not be healthy enough, or some other problems might hold him back. Stallone was aware that everything has its time. He knew that **life does not wait on us**.

In the book of Ecclesiastes in the Bible, King Solomon explains that life is our opportunity to grow and to reach our potential. He asserts that throughout our lives we encounter various trials and challenges that ultimately determine what kind of people we become. We can see life as a learning experience, or we can resist life and believe that we are somehow supposed to have everything easy while we are here.

In John 7:6, Jesus Christ is aware that his life is on a certain schedule. Whenever he is approached about taking certain actions, Jesus says, "The time for me has not yet come." Jesus was aware that his life had a certain sense of destiny about it.

Are we putting off writing that book or song, going after that job, spending more time with our children, asking that special someone out, encouraging someone who needs some help, or telling someone that we love them? Do we realize that our lives have a purpose and that we have a destiny even if we do not realize it? **Do we realize that time is running out on us?**

We get one chance at life. Use that chance wisely.

Decide What To Do With Your Life

I want you to know that no matter who you are, you **can live a more fulfilling life--no matter what anyone tells you**. I don't care what you have done in the past. You may have made unwise remarks, you may have taken actions so thoughtless that you could never live them down, you may have embarrassed yourself by going overboard trying to meet romantic partners--or you may feel totally humiliated by the life you have lived so far. But I am telling you--it**'s not the past but the future that matters! The past is gone.** What are you going to do with your life? **It's not a question; it's THE question.**

What Makes Life Exciting?

Life is exciting because we know that this very moment could be our last. Not knowing what's going to happen next is what drives us forward. When we step outside of our fears, we can begin to see life for what it really is. It's not about pleasing other people; it's about being the people that we were meant to be. It is about being the warrior, the princess, the athlete, or the player.

Don't Die At 50 And Be Buried At 80

Don't live in the past, basing everything on what you've already done. Age gracefully. **Live now!**

Many people feel that their time has already passed. They live on past memories of how good (or bad) life was when they were young. They feel that if only life could be the way it was when they were growing up then the world would be a happy place.

Past memories and past history are very exciting and interesting, but each phase of history and time is only part of the mystery of life. We have to take history as a whole rather than take a particular slice of time and decide that particular time was the best. We have to accept and live in the time period in which we were born.

We do not know exactly what direction history is going to take because people determine what happens on Earth. The choices that we make determine the kind of future we are going to have.

To live meaningful lives, we should accept each day for what it is and do our part to make life better for others. It is discouraging to feel that the best part of our lives is behind us when the real truth is that the best part may be ahead. We just don't know. If we give up and resign ourselves to just passing time until we die, we may live in 30 or 40 more years of misery.

Live life fully everyday.

Accept Yourself As You Are Because You Are Incredible

I want to restate the point I made earlier: It is critically important that we accept ourselves as we are. You may be a slim and gorgeous woman who makes all the guys' hearts flutter. You may be the handsome guy that every woman in the world wants to be with. You may be a rather average person with average abilities and average looks. You may have taken a walk through hell and no on Earth could ever understand what you've been through.

Please consider carefully what I'm about to say to you. **The great challenge of life is for us to accept ourselves and the role we were born into. Once we do this, we will have found the secret that everyone is searching for. Go for it, my friend. You get to live one time—give it everything you've got!**

Experiencing Life Right Now

Life consists of different experiences at different times. I wrote the following poem, *Right Now*, to capture the feelings and happenings of any given point in time.

Right now someone is laughing and someone is crying

At this moment someone is lonely and someone
else is being adored

During this minute someone is happy and
someone is sad

Presently someone is depressed and someone
else is extremely content

Right now someone is dying and someone else
is being born

So go the moments of life.

Life is a collection of feelings, passions, desires, and challenges. For us to feel less than or better than someone else is really an illusion, because each of us experiences time from moment to moment. **No one person has a monopoly on happiness.**

Allow Change To Happen To Us

Most of us go through significant changes as we get older. For example, I have seen people who cared very little for religion in their early years become very spiritual in their later years.

To keep from throwing away our one shot at life, it is helpful to **allow the possibility** for change into our lives. When we are 25 we don't know how we are going to feel at age 55. If we are not willing to be open-minded to life and tolerant of new situations, we are destined to stay the way we are and to possibly miss tremendous life rewards we may have otherwise gotten. It is possible that we could grow old as cynical, resentful, and intolerant people.

When former President of the United States, Ronald

Reagan, died, his funeral was more of a celebration of life rather than a somber affair. Reagan was 69 years old when he became president, and he brought a vitality to the office that perhaps no other president ever had. President Reagan was humorous and optimistic. He made people feel good about being Americans. He enjoyed life and he was comfortable with himself. On the first day of his presidency, he got goose bumps and he did not mind saying so.

Our world is a kind of stage on which we are playing out our lives. Much too often, we take everything too seriously. We are only going to pass through this world one time, yet we often allow our perceptions of what we think life is to keep us from having the experience we really want. We get back in life what we focus on the most. If we focus daily on the idea that life is a dull, uninteresting experience, life will become monotonous to us.

We can undermine our own happiness by focusing on these average thoughts. We don't let ourselves see how good life could be. We decide that we know how life is, and we begin to block out new thoughts, attitudes, and beliefs. Eventually we are so far gone that many of our thoughts and behaviors are little more than habits. We stop dreaming. Our main goal may become just getting through each day with occasional moments of pleasure.

The Most Important Part Of This Book

Please understand that our minds can be in a fog. We can think that everything is okay when in reality we are 1000 light years from the truth. Our children may be suffering the consequences of our negative behaviors. Our spouses and friends may be suffering the consequences of our behaviors.

We have got to be willing to humble ourselves and begin seeing life as it really is. It's time to stop playing games. People are counting on us! The cemeteries are full of people who chose to live the kind of lives they thought they should live. Many of these people had very little positive influence on their world.

Now is the time to be a better husband, wife, mother, father, son, daughter, or friend. Be open to making some new decisions now, before it's too late.

When we lose the power to make logical decisions, we are really headed for trouble. When we get to a point where we are more concerned with our own desires over our families, friends, and jobs, we are really walking down a dangerous street.

Try to reflect on the ideas in this book. All of us are different. There is no absolute, standard set of answers that will work for all of us. The martial arts expert, Bruce Lee, often asserted that there is no set style of fighting because every fight is different and unpredictable. In the same way, all of us have different backgrounds and different challenges. So, be flexible as you read this book. Resolve to make some kind of change that will start you down a more successful road in life. Be aware that what you and I hold to be the true may not actually be the truth.

If at times you feel alone, desperate, and disconnected, your life may be giving you some signals that you are not in harmony with reality. The Bible story of "The Prodigal Son" is about a young man who decides to leave his father and go out to live the pleasurable, worldly life. Ultimately the man's fortune turns, he runs out of money, and he has no place to turn. Life itself has taught the man a lesson. The Bible says, "When he came to his senses," he returned to his father, who actually represents God, and his father welcomed him with open arms because the son had come to his senses.

Do we need to come to our senses? The example of the lost son helps us see that we can be spiritually blind to what is truly going on. **It takes a lot of courage for us to realize that we might not be on the right track.**

Some Of Us Have
A Mountain To Climb

I am convinced that many of us have a more difficult time in life than others. It does not really matter why. Some of us have grown up with certain challenges and really do have a mountain to climb. But for those who are willing to climb the mountain, the rewards are sweet and bountiful.

Let the ideas and thoughts in this book help you pursue your dreams. You get one shot at life. Give life your best effort. Let today be a turning point. Life is not easy for any of us. But those who are able to rise above themselves receive uncommon rewards.

The Loneliest Feeling In The World

There is no feeling worse than the feeling of hopeless-ness. When we feel hopeless, we have no reason for living. Life is a kind of empty existence that is hard to describe. If you have been there, you know what I mean.

Consider that all we really are besides our physical bod-ies are our feelings. We exist in the here and now. Everything that happens to us is going on in our minds. If our minds are on the wrong channel, our feelings are working against us.

If you are feeling hopeless, you have probably lost your perspective on life. Our minds are able to experience life on thousands of different levels because we are free to think about whatever we want to think about. Try to realize that nothing really means anything in and of itself. It is the meaning that we give to people, situations, and events that determine how we see reality.

If you are feeling hopeless, try to back off from the situation at hand and see if you can get a better perspective on your feelings. There are reasons why you feel the way you do and most of the reasons come from experiences from your past that have caused you to have certain beliefs. **Until you change or confront these beliefs, you are destined to live out of your subconscious thoughts.** And you will go through life thinking it is fate.

If you are unable to overcome your feelings of hopelessness, have the courage to seek professional help.

Life Is Right Now

Living right now means perceiving the moments of life as they really are rather than through the filter of our own ideas, notions, and opinions. It means slowing down and getting past our internal voice. If we are not careful, we will not really experience life because we will be too busy experiencing our subjective opinion of what we think life is about.

It is interesting to look at how we perceive ourselves. We try to find some kind of significance in various pursuits. For example, a great surgeon may find his greatest meaning by thinking about what a great surgeon he is. And that is okay.

However, if my son needs a highly esteemed surgeon immediately and the aforementioned surgeon suddenly dies, I am going to get another surgeon and so would you. The meaning in our lives is not completely dependent on who or what we think we are.

Don't misunderstand me. I am grateful that we have great surgeons. It's just that if the meaning in our lives is determined by who we think we are, we may be living a dull existence. There is so much more to life than thinking we are valuable simply because we hold a certain position. In Matthew 6:27, Jesus Christ said, "Which of you, by taking thought, can add one cubit unto his stature?"

Sometimes we may see life from such a narrow focus that we don't give ourselves enough mental room to consider what life is really about. For example, if we happen to die today, the meaning in our lives will be whatever meaning we have given it until our demise. Even at my age, I see life differently every day. I learn something new every day.

In other words, there is a possibility that we could miss life because we are looking so hard for life. Instead of letting life happen to us, we may be trying to create some role, identity, position, ideal, or vision of what **we think life should be**.

It is paramount that we realize that time is getting away from us. We simply don't have the time and luxury to be wrong about what the meaning of life is. **Be alive. Don't be hypnotized by your notions of what you think life should be. Life it what it is. You and I are just players on the stage of the universe. Be passionate. You are not going to be here forever.**

Don't Be Too Rich Or Too Poor

Living a meaningful life involves having the financial freedom to make choices. We should strive to have financial freedom. People in the middle class usually have more options about with what do to with their lives. The extremely wealthy are often limited by traditions and other pressures. The poor are usually deprived of education and economic advantages.

When we have some financial freedom, we are better able to be creative and to give something unique to society. We are better able to enjoy life because life is more fun and fulfilling.

We should focus on doing whatever it takes to have financial freedom: go to school, learn some skills, take more risks, make new friends, branch out. We need to resolve within ourselves that we will do whatever it takes to have financial freedom and the self-reliance to pursue an exciting life. Life can be great, but many people have never gotten to the point where they can see just how good life can be.

Realize That *All* Of Us Struggle With Discovering Who We Are And What We Want To Be

To find more meaning in life, realize that every one of us struggles to find our identity and our purpose. All of us have powerful illusions in our teens and twenties that what we think we want to do and be is the absolute answer to life for us. However, as we get older, we begin to see that what we thought was the secret of life was somewhat of a delusion or mistaken notion. Young people go after all kinds of ventures in an effort to "find" themselves. However, they simply don't know how they are going to feel 10, 20, or 30 years later.

Trying to find some kind of significance, yet having the wisdom to know what will really make us happy as we journey through life, is a delicate balancing act, especially for young people. We should seek guidance from wise, older people who are truly happy because they have reflected on the meaning of life. **We will be growing until we die. It takes time to understand ourselves and life. Life does not ever stay the same.**

We need to understand that all of us feel inadequate when we are young. We try to appear to be confident, appealing, and courageous, but under all the acting are people who feel very insecure about themselves and the future. Bullies are the most insecure people in the world.

There Is No One Way To Find Meaning

People who live the most meaningful and exciting lives realize that there is no one set role or way to be. People who live meaningful lives are spontaneous, curious, funny, compassionate, flirtatious, playful, spiritual, exciting, kind, helpful to others, tolerant, and nutty. They bring so much to the lives of everyone around them. They help others and they spend time with children. They try to make the world a better place rather than feeling like a victim of life. They work hard to overcome the obstacles that life has given them. They know that they are here for a reason and that their lives have purpose. They don't need other people to determine their value and worth. They don't lose interest in life. They realize that every day is a new adventure. **They fully realize that**

they get one chance at life--and that chance is right now.

There is no one secret to success. We become successful when we make things happen by setting goals and working hard to achieve them. Even famous people were once regular people like you and me.

Chuck Norris, the movie star and karate champion, was very shy growing up. His family was very poor and he had an alcoholic father who was not a good role model. His mother taught him to have a strong faith in God. Chuck joined the Air Force after he left high school and he learned karate while serving in Korea. He worked hard and ultimately became a six-time World Professional Middle Weight Karate Champion. But this was only the beginning.

Chuck became friends with Bruce Lee, Steve McQueen, James Coburn, Kareem Abdul Jabbar, and many other celebrities. Chuck started making movies and he starred in *Walker, Texas Ranger*, which ran for eight years on CBS. Today Chuck is still a very spiritual man, and he considers his greatest accomplishment the Kick Drugs Out of America Foundation, a program to help kids with their self-esteem and to help keep them off drugs.

To live a meaningful life like Chuck Norris, we need to give value to ourselves. Have you ever noticed a film clip of people in prison? Often, the inmates have a look on their faces that says, "We deserve to be here. We are not as good as other people, so we deserve whatever treatment we get in life. The mistakes that we made are worse than other people's mistakes. It does not really matter what you do to us because we are the lower crust in society." Their self-esteem and self-concept is so low that they just accept what comes their way.

Many of us have such an attitude and we are not in

prison. We have learned to see ourselves from such a depressing point of view that we hold ourselves back from being the people we have the capability to be. We may feel that we were just meant to lose at the game of life and that is just the way it is.

Are We Going To Be Ordinary Or Extraordinary People?

Many of us consider ourselves ordinary people. When famous people come to town, we stand in line for hours waiting to get their autographs. But instead of being ordinary, why couldn't we be extraordinary?

All of us yearn to do something that matters. It's the truth. Face it. All of us want to accomplish something and be noticed. Bruce Lee and Chuck Norris both **wanted** to be in movies. When we are not honest about what we want, and when we do not diligently go after it, our lives become boring, routine and **ordinary**.

All of the time life is teaching us, we just don't realize it. We reach certain ages and we think we have it figured out, not realizing that we are just scratching the surface of what life is about.

We may graduate from college in our twenties and get a decent job. We may be promoted and get married and have a child and all the while be thinking we have it all figured out. We may pursue all sorts of avenues of adventure: music, art, writing, alcohol, drugs, marriage, fame, travel, all the while thinking that the roads we choose are the right roads, because we have it figured out. We know the secret. We may look at the pathetic masses with a superficial sympathy for they have no idea what is going on. And all the while, we are the pathetic ones, because just about the time we think that we have life figured out, life is going to throw us a knockout punch. **Why would we need to live the rest of our lives if we knew all the answers in our twenties and thirties?**

We were born into a certain point in history. Many centuries have already passed. We are only part of the story. There were many chapters in the story before we got here. We are only a pebble in the stream of life. **Life is not about us--it's about all of us.**

Building Character

We need to be honest with ourselves. Are we building true character in ourselves, our children, and others, or are we doing our own thing, creating our own philosophy, and just hoping everything will somehow work out?

Get the edge in your life by emulating successful people. Our lives are not measured in years but in what we have accomplished and how many people's lives we have made a difference in.

We Think Most About What We Really Want

Outwardly some of us claim that we want to be happy, yet we go around feeling mad, depressed, and resentful. To other people we claim that we want success and happiness, but we don't recognize that we are doing very little to gain happiness. Our subconscious deceives us.

Please think carefully about what I am about to say. In

our hearts, all of us want to be happy. The reason I know this is I have never seen anyone who has not experienced at least a few minutes of joy and laughter. Occasionally we expose our good feelings, even if we are determined to be angry, hateful, and resentful about life. Our real self gives us away. No matter how much we may think that we hate ourselves, life, and other people, down deep inside we want to be happy. We want to matter. We want to be significant. The sad thing is that we can actually *learn* to be miserable. And being miserable and not caring for life may get us by for a while, but sooner or later we are going to pay the piper because this is real life; this is not some product of our imagination that we are living in. It may happen when we are on our death bed, or during the loss of a loved one, or in the middle of some tragedy or disaster. **We suddenly come to our senses and realize we were not the people we should have been. We realize how many people we could have helped and how much happier we could have been if we had tried harder.**

As I said earlier, many of us have walked through hell. But the question is, are we going to let our past experiences cause us to resent life and people, or are we going to rise above ourselves and create some kind of meaning in life...for ourselves and others?

What Really Holds Us Back From Living Meaningful Lives?

Why are so many people unable to live meaningful lives? First, they don't understand what life is about. They don't understand the point or purpose of life. So their lives are confusing, like playing a game that has no rules. How can anyone play a game without knowing what the rules are?

So even though they don't understand life, these people make up rules to live by. Because of their rules, sometimes they win and sometimes they lose. Their lives are confusing. Their lives are often in conflict with reality because they have no steadfast foundation on which to base their lives. They just go through life taking whatever is thrown at them rather than trying to understand life.

We can find success in life by building our lives on steadfast principles of success rather than on our own notions of what we think will bring us success. **As we have said, there are certain laws of success that will always work and to depart from these basic laws is to invite trouble.**

What Is The Purpose Of Life?

The purpose of life is for us to realize our own uniqueness and for us to do what we were put here to do. All of us are here for a reason. **We are not an accident**, but we have to search out our particular purpose. Along the way we encounter challenges, some negative and some positive, that help us grow and find our way. Everything that happens to us shows us another aspect of ourselves. For most of us, the richest meaning in our lives comes from serving others in some capacity and thereby helping the world to be a better place. Serving others does not mean that we sacrifice our own happiness. Life is fun and interesting. We need to take care of our own mental, physical, and psychological needs or we will feel deprived, weak or lacking.

We should be careful not to let the distractions of life such as television and worldly pleasures deceive us into thinking that we are living meaningful lives. The trivial amusements of the world can burn a lot of time off our life clocks and cause us not to pursue and notice more important and fulfilling events.

We should focus on the meaning that we give to the events in our lives. Life is not just some meaningless happening. The daily events of life and the way we respond to those events determine what kind of people we become. **Understanding that the events in our lives happen for a reason will help us find meaning in the present moment.** For example, if a man opens a door for a woman, one woman might think the guy is putting her below him thinking that she can't open the door for herself. Another woman might think that he is just trying to get in good with her. Another may really appreciate the kindness. The point is that all of us interpret events in different ways. **The key to finding meaning is interpreting the events of our lives with the aim of finding meaning in our lives.** What does the event mean? What can I learn about myself from this event? What can I learn about other people? Asking these questions requires us to raise our awareness, rather than just always responding to events with knee-jerk responses based on our past feelings, and the needs of our egos.

Crossing The Bridge
To A Meaningful Life

Picture a bridge that is between a vast wilderness and a tropical paradise. The wilderness is where we are and the tropical paradise is where we would like to be. We have lived in the wilderness all our lives and it is fairly comfortable for us. Our needs are met, we have some fun, and life is bearable.

But the tropical paradise looks very inviting and from time to time we fantasize about living there. But we know that the bridge is old and spans a deep gorge. It could be difficult, even dangerous to cross the bridge. Why risk taking a chance since we are doing fairly well here in the wilderness? It probably would not be worth the risks to try and cross over to the land we dream about.

The analogy of the bridge helps us to see where we may be. Perhaps we have read books similar to this one and we know that at least some of the information makes sense. But, because of our general level of comfort and our apprehension about trying new things, we stay where we are. We know that if we made some changes, we might actually feel good about ourselves and that could be a strange feeling. People would start treating us differently and that would make us feel awkward. People would probably expect more from us and that may not be what we want.

We know in our hearts that we can do better, but we just can't let go and make ourselves cross the bridge because we're scared that people might put us down, too much may be expected from us, it's too risky, or we are just more content where we are than we realize.

Every day of our lives we stand on the wilderness side of the bridge and we occasionally glance over to the tropical paradise. But, we turn away and go through our ordinary day once again because it feels the safest. We think that maybe some day we will cross the bridge, *but not today*. Our learned habits and emotions are controlling us. Even though the daily demands of life seem critically important, this could be our last day on Earth and then none of these things would matter whatsoever.

When we live in the past or dwell on the future, there is little time to think about the present. The present moment is all there is. There is nothing else. Nothing.

Cross that bridge.

Develop The Courage To Live

I urge you to come to the realization that everyone walking the face of the Earth is a little bit different. All of us have our secret agenda, our personal desires, and our particular ways of looking at life. This is just human nature.

It is important to come to this realization about people if we are going to be courageous enough to live life on our terms. All of us came from different backgrounds and all of had different experiences. If we lack courage because we feel that we are not like other people, we are holding ourselves back. Everyone has doubts at times.

It takes courage to accomplish anything in this life. Even a child is known for whether or not he stands up for himself. Courage is the virtue that separates average people from the best.

Not having the courage to live our own lives is the biggest mistake we can make in life. **Courage is at the core of success,** and all of us have more courage than we realize.

Get In The Game

When a football team is behind seven points in the fourth quarter with only a few seconds left on the clock, **someone has to take control of the situation**. Someone has to have the guts to make the tough calls. The same holds true in life.

We get one chance at life, so we need to make the most of our situation. To be successful in life we have to develop a winning edge to help us make the tough calls. Too many people spend their lives on the sidelines and never become players.

This is your life. Go for it! You may not win, but you must try. You have got to be in the game.

Nobody completely understands the game of life. But, if you are not even in the game, you may be missing out on great people, self-fulfillment, fun, meaning, and the chance to serve others.

Take Action Daily To Make Your Dreams Come True

Most of us have goals, ideals, and aspirations. For example, we may want to write a book, go to college, get married, or be an athlete. However, these goals are only guiding thoughts and general ideas that we aim toward. We still have to live daily, moment-to- moment in life, no matter what our desires and wishes are.

If we spend a lot of time wondering why our dreams are not coming true, we may not be living the kind of life from minute to minute to make our dreams come true. This can be very frustrating. We may be telling our friends and families that we are going to write a book or paint a portrait, but until we write the book or paint the portrait, we are really just wishing and hoping.

It is helpful to live in such a way that we do something *daily* to help us make our dreams and goals become reality. If not, we can become frustrated because realistically our desires are just wishful thinking. **We must move forward and accomplish something toward our goals every day.** Otherwise we may become like an aspiring writer who can't write the first line of a book because he believes that every line he writes has to be the greatest thing ever written in the universe. Can you see the pseudo-grandeur and unreality of this kind of writer's life?

Our lives become much more meaningful, fun, and gratifying when we take action to make our dreams come true.

Find More Success By Overcoming Boredom And Apathy

When I was a teenager, there was not much to do in southwest Georgia on a muggy, hot, August night except sit on the front porch or watch one of the three programs on television. Boredom would come on like a junkyard dog attacking an intruder in a used car lot. I decided that I had to learn to overcome boredom or I would end up living a dull, uninteresting life.

Ultimately, I started spending more time reading, interacting with people, participating in sports, and helping others. Within a short time I was no longer bored.

People who win at life learn to overcome boredom. They come to understand that life is too fascinating to be boring. They learn to value themselves for who they are. They don't let themselves live in a world of "poor me" forever. Somewhere along the line they come to understand how precious and meaningful their lives are. **So they rise above boredom.**

My friend, I am reaching out to you with my soul telling you there is more; there is much more going on than

you may realize. Wake up and have some fun. You are part of the reason that this world exists. You don't need someone to tell you whether or not you matter. **You matter, period.**

Find Success By Overcoming The Perils Of The Past

I am not trying to just build you up in an unrealistic way. I am someone who lived with low self-esteem for years who did not care whether he lived or died. But I learned to understand that whether we live in Africa, the United States, or China, we are part of a plan that the creator of the universe has put together. It is very difficult to completely understand what is going on in the universe, but as I said earlier, none of us completely understands.

Even though we may never completely understand the universe, we do understand that if we can become victorious over our negative feelings such as poor self-esteem, self-doubts, or cynical attitudes, we can learn to live very satisfying lives. **Remember, what would anything mean....if we were not here?** Life is going on in our minds. Make the decision to turn your life experience into a positive one.

You may say, "But I **am** the one exception, you simply do not understand the hell I have been through." I feel for you as I feel for myself. **But what good will it do anybody for you to throw your life away because your past was so ugly?** What good does it do you or anyone else to spend the rest of your life being depressed? Is that how you want to be remembered? Do you want people to say that you spent your one shot at life being depressed?

Forgive my arrogance, I just want so much for you to

live with passion because you are my brothers and sisters on this planet....and I love all of you. I want all of you to win.

Not convinced yet that you are a diamond in the world? Well, let's keep reasoning together. **Hang in there!**

Find Success By Conquering The Ego

When we allow our opinion of ourselves to control us, we are not living the best life possible. Our ego is the part of us that constantly compares ourselves to others. The ego is usually either looking at the future or the past. When we focus too much on anxieties, anticipations, or ambitions, we are living in the future and missing the wisdom of what we could be learning in the moment.

When we focus on anger, self-pity, condemnation of others, and envy, we are actually living in the past so we are not able to see the present moment clearly or to make wise decisions based on what the present moment is trying to show us or teach us. Growth is only possible when we begin to let go of some of the expressions of the ego.

It is helpful to learn to accept life as it is. To resist reality is like resisting the turning of the Earth. When we really begin to let go of the false pride and power that has held us back in life, we can then really begin to see ourselves as we really are. We can begin to focus on the higher thoughts in life such as humility, self-acceptance, respect for others, tolerance, self-control, patience, kindness, and love for ourselves and others.

All the great teachers throughout all of history have taught that we take on the attributes of whatever we focus our attention on. **Whatever we think about, we become.**

Now, let's put all of this in more simple terms. All of us have learned to deal with life in a certain way. We may not always like the way we handle life, but at least it helps us survive. Some of us go through life down on ourselves. We have been focused for so long on thoughts of how little we have to offer that we have literally become people who feel we have little to offer. Other people have used forceful ways such as aggression and intimidation to get through life. So they have become forceful people. And there are literally thousands of variations in the ways people behave.

Please consider the following statements very carefully. **We are made in such a way that we can experience life on millions of levels. We may actually believe that the life we are now living is the only one possible for us. We may limit what we can do and accomplish in life by living our lives in a kind of bubble. We may not realize that our particular bubble is one tiny bubble in a vast universe. We may not allow ourselves to see the possibilities in our lives because we already know that the life we are living is the only one possible so how can other influences or new thoughts penetrate our bubble?**

My friend, time is running out. Are you happy? Are you living the kind of life that you want to live? If not, take some kind of action today that will start you down a new road. If you have a negative self-image, work hard to overcome it. Awaken to the life you could be living. Be open-minded. Life is very complex, and none of us completely understands what life is about.

You get one chance at life. **Are you throwing the dice and waiting to see what number comes up, or are you taking charge, developing your personal power, planning, being**

open to new possibilities, and allowing the creator of the universe to work through you?

The True Secret Of Success Is Love

Please understand that the bottom line to life is love. Everybody gets hungry. Everybody hurts. Everybody needs others. Everybody needs love. The more love we give, the more meaningful our lives will be.

Children pick up the habits of the adults. If adults love others, children will love others. If adults hate others, children will hate others. If adults are narrow-minded, children will be narrow-minded. If the adults are terrorists, the children will be terrorists.

Love is the answer.

Find Success By Realizing That All Of Us Struggle With Insecurities

We don't often hear what other people are truly feeling and thinking about. It is helpful to understand that there are many, many people struggling emotionally as they go through life. I'm talking about people who appear to have it all together. For example, I heard a very intelligent lady say that she is "addicted to shame." She asserted that she could even have this feeling for no reason. "It's 11:00 p. m. on Saturday night and I feel ashamed to exist."

I have heard many other people talk about how they have let others use them and determine how they feel about themselves. When people treated them badly, they blamed themselves. When relationships went sour, it was somehow their fault. When other people taught them to feel ashamed of themselves, they grew into adulthood feeling ashamed and unworthy to live a vibrant life.

The point here is that it is not unusual for any of us to have bad thoughts about ourselves. We are not **the only one** who has all the bad thoughts. Life is so complex that many of us develop insecurities and doubt ourselves and our ability to function normally in society.

It is comforting to realize that all of us struggle emotionally in many ways. None of us have some kind of hard shell that shields us from the world and its arrows. Realizing this fact alone can give us *hope* that we have as much chance to live a meaningful life as anyone else. It's when we feel that **we alone** are suffering that we begin to detach ourselves from the world--and we end up living in our own little private universe.

It is also helpful to realize that we do not determine how other people act. We can only determine how we are going to relate to the world.

Discover Success
Through Positive Relationships

We have discussed why the world is the way it is. We have considered various ways to find meaning in life. We have looked at what we can do to develop a winning edge and to find success in life. Now we want to examine another important aspect of lives: our relationships. Most people desire to have fulfilling relationships. Life can be rather lonely if we are by ourselves a lot, even if we really have our act together. Most people want to know that someone special cares for them simply for who they are. All of us want to have close family relationships. All of us need friends to help us experience the richness of this marvelous experience we call life.

In this section, we are going to look at some ways that we can improve our relationships. We will consider how we can find more romance, excitement, and genuine friendships that will make our lives more fun and meaningful.

Understanding Relationships

One aspect of life that can be difficult to handle is wanting something so badly we can taste it, yet not being able to get it. This particularly holds true for relationships. We see someone who we know could make all our dreams come true, yet at some point it becomes obvious that the person is not going to be in our life. This has got to be one of the most frustrating situations in life. Of course there are other things we may want badly such as houses, cars, money, our team to win, a better body, our political party to be in power, and so on. But I think that wanting someone we can't have is at the top of the list.

There are lots of ramifications to not having the person we want. We feel we have to settle for someone "less." We may feel that we don't measure up to other men and women. We may feel second-rate. We may feel an indescribable emptiness that comes from knowing that we have actually got to live in this world without that special person.

I have learned a lot about not getting to be with certain other people. First, I think that other people do not realize how great we are. When you get through laughing, we will continue. We tend to see life through a kind of tunnel vision. We think that if a man or woman looks or acts a certain way that he (or she) has just got to be the person for us. We often do not consider our personality differences. Is the person into some of the same things we are? Do we consider how the person might look in a few years? Will the person treat us with respect and dignity? Is the person someone who will make us proud? Does the person care for other people in the world? Does the person go after deep spiritual goals or does he or she just live for pleasure in the here and now?

Now I realize that some of what I am saying may seem trite and old-fashioned, but I am looking back over 50 years of living. I know when I fell in love with that girl in the first grade everything I just said would have been meaningless to me. But it is all true. Once we get locked into one person, our life is locked to go a certain direction. It is helpful to question our own motives. Why do we want a particular person so much? Will he or she make us look good in front of others by being an attractive ornament wrapped around our arm? Are our feelings mainly sexually motivated? Are we thinking that the person can make our disappointing life more meaningful? Don't get me wrong. These are not bad reasons to want someone. It's just that the bottom line is that there are lots of cool people in the world who we may be missing out on if we are totally focused on one person. Focusing on one person that we may not be able to have makes life depressing. And the truth is, that person can't truly make us happy anyway. We make our own selves happy.

The bottom line is that if we are depressed about life because we can't have someone we want, we are probably causing ourselves a lot of unnecessary grief. We are probably being too narrowly focused in one direction and we may be blaming life for our unpleasant feelings when the truth is we may need to get a broader perspective. There are lots of cool men and women. We truly have no idea what each new person could bring into our lives--because we don't "know" them. We should be looking around more and enjoying ourselves more. Remember, our value and self-worth truly comes from within. **Having all the toys in the world will not make us happy if we are not happy with ourselves on the inside.**

Find Success By Being Interested In Other People

Mary was a lovely lady with a million dollar smile. Everyone thought she was attractive, so Mary never had a problem getting a date or meeting new friends. Everybody wanted to be around Mary and she knew it. But Mary had a problem and she did not know that she had a problem. The problem with Mary was that she saw herself as a lovely woman with a million dollar smile who never had a problem getting a date or meeting new friends. Mary played the "role" of the popular, lovely woman.

While there was nothing wrong with the way Mary saw herself, Mary did not fully realize that the way she saw herself and the way she interacted with life determined her degree of happiness. If her goal was to be an attractive, popular woman, she succeeded. If her goal was to understand other people and life in a deeper way, she may have missed out on life some. Mary did not know what it was like to be the underdog, to be unpopular, to be poor, or to be put down by other people. Mary did not understand why some people resent life. Mary probably could not understand why some women let themselves go because they have been put down and avoided for so long that they don't even care anymore. Mary may not have understood why certain people spend their lives helping the poor, the sick, the disabled, and the downtrodden. Though Mary was very popular and most people responded to her favorably, she could not understand why her life seemed empty. It was because Mary thought that looks and popularity were the secrets of life.

If we show a lot of interest in other people, we are going to have many friends. But if we are too self-absorbed, it will show up in such ways as depression, irritability, discomfort, uneasiness, and having bad days sometimes without understanding why. We cannot deceive life. There are central truths in this life that are going to haunt us if we do not try to see life for what it is rather than what we want it to be.

Let's consider Marty. Marty is not the best-looking guy around, but Marty does believe in himself. People like him because he is authentic and real. Marty wants to understand people and the world. He is not preoccupied with his own agenda. Marty knows he is just a speck in a vast universe so he searches diligently for wisdom, understanding, and meaning. He understands that there are many, many people on earth who see life differently than he does. Marty's curiosity and his desire to understand others bring much meaning into his life. His days are exciting and dynamic because he realizes what an awesome and complicated world we live in. He looks forward to each day to see what new idea or revelation he might experience.

Mary's emphasis on looks and popularity crowded out

other important ideas, reflections, and pursuits. But there are hundreds of thoughts, actions, and behaviors that can keep us from living a more rewarding life. Some of these include: being down on ourselves, thinking too highly of ourselves, believing only in our philosophy of life, being too religious, not being spiritual enough, being preoccupied with certain interests, having an "I don't care" attitude, having a cynical attitude, living in fear, focusing too much on our own self-interests without regard to the feelings of others, and so on. Anything that blocks our efforts to grow, change and take a more realistic view of life can keep us from living a more rewarding life.

Confidence Is A Major Key To Finding Success

Some people hamper their possibilities for successful relationships. They have signs hanging on them that say, "I'm not very interesting, so don't consider spending time with me unless you don't have anything else in the world to do." So the world responds to them that way. It's a scenario that some people play out their entire lives and they never come to understand why life isn't more fun.

When we act more confidently, when we act like we matter, when we laugh more often, when we look people in the eyes, when we act more interesting, we look better. We are more appealing. We catch people's attention more quickly. Men and women are more apt to notice us. This is true with everyone. **You are not the exception to the rule because there are no exceptions!**

It is so important that we present a good impression to

the world, because people are watching us. Remember, each moment of life is simply an experience. We tend to see life as something that is going to happen, but life is happening right now. Try not to focus on what might be or could be or what you wish for. Focus on being a more appealing person **right now.**

In reality, there are no average people. If we think we are average, we are simply deceiving ourselves, and we are causing ourselves to look like and act like we are average. Do you see? **You must begin seeing the precious human being that you are because if you don't, you are holding yourself back and hurting your one shot at life!**

It's time to unlearn some of our negative behaviors so we can have some fun for a change. The days, weeks, and months are slowly passing by. We must see ourselves and life in a bigger way. We are getting back from life exactly what we are giving. Think about it. Are you giving people a chance to see the best in you? Smile more, act silly, wear cool clothes, be friendly, be sexy, be cool, be **YOUR UNIQUE SELF.** Stop thinking that you can't do it. That is your problem! The world can see that you think you are not cool. **Your thoughts are showing!**

We make choices and decisions everyday. The choices we make on any given day build on the choices and decisions we made on the previous day, and on and on. These choices and decisions determine who we are and what we become. If at some point in life we do not like the person we have become, **we can change our choices and change the direction of our lives.**

I spent a large part of my life being down on myself, and I know that I missed thousands of good and meaningful moments. When I finally started making some changes in my life, my whole world changed. When I improved my self-image, developed more confidence, and learned to have a more optimistic attitude, every area of my life got better.

The future is not a mystery. What happens to us in the future is going to be determined by what we are doing right now. Every thought we have sends us in a different direction. Think of all the choices we make: whether or not to go to college, whether to date or settle down, whether to pursue goals or to sit around and watch TV, whether to make some changes or stay the same. Actually, we are free to take our life any direction we want to take it except for the limitations we have already placed on ourselves.

If we are miserable right now, we need to do something different! We cannot keep acting the same way and expect anything to change.

The Illusion Of Happiness

As we get older, we are better able to look back on our lives and see how we did. As I think back over my life, I realize that I had many failures or at least situations that did not turn out rosy. I have had problems with close friends that marred our relationships forever. I have known girls that I wanted so badly that I would have given them the moon, yet they often could not understand me and they went after other pursuits. I lived much of my life with weakness and low self-esteem and I often escaped from life through drugs and alcohol.

Now that I look back, I can see more clearly that some of the happiness I was after was somewhat of an illusion. I will explain. All of us have certain needs, wants, and desires. Seldom do our desires completely match the desires of others. If we are not careful, we will roll along trying to get our needs met without realizing that the other people in our lives are not quite on the same channel we are on. All of a sudden, it is too late to make things right. The relationship becomes "what it is" or "what it was" and eventually it becomes just a memory.

Think about some of the relationships you have had so far in your life. Is there anything you would have done differently if you had it to go over? Is there anything you could do now to make your relationships better? This is your life. This day will only be a memory tomorrow. Be aware that all of us are imperfect and sometimes we let our imperfections come between us and our pursuit of relationships. All of us operate out of self-interest to a strong degree even more than we realize. In relationships, whether with boyfriends, girlfriends, family, or friends, there is a lot of mutual understanding that needs to take place if the relationships are going to be successful. We cannot totally know what other people are thinking or feeling. We can get a lot of mileage, though, out of letting our friends and families know how much they mean to us.

Happiness is somewhat of an illusion. What we think will make us happy today, **MAY NOT BE WHAT MAKES US HAPPY IN THE FUTURE.** Our background, families, other people, and the condition of the world have a tremendous bearing on what we **THINK WILL MAKE US HAPPY.**

What Will Be
The Ending To Your Story?

If we could jump to the end of our lives and look back, how would we evaluate the kind of lives we lived?

What would we say about our lives? Could we profess that our children turned out well? Could we say that life was a fascinating adventure? Could we assert that we made a real difference in the world? Could any of us claim that we gave life our all? The real question is: Were we champions or did we hang out on the sidelines?

Your story can have a happy ending if you spend your time pursuing success. The true elements of success are: examining our own lives, loving others, courage, enthusiasm, hard work, persistence, taking risks, being responsible, doing our best, and learning from failure.

The rewards of success are joy, peace, and happiness.

OUESTIONS TO PONDER

- What makes any given day important? Is any day more important than any other day?

- Why is it important to believe that there are many possibilities in our lives?

- Name some ways that we can live more fulfilling lives by realizing that our time is limited.

- If you knew that you had only one week to live, how would you spend your time?

- Is there anything to be gained by giving up on life as we get older?

- What is the purpose of your life?

- What actions can you take to make yourself more appealing?

- What can you do to improve your relationships?

CHAPTER TWELVE

What if We Have Really Messed Up?

ave you ever really made a bad mistake? Have you done something that you have regretted your whole life? Maybe you looked bad in front of a crowd, stole someone's property, committed adultery, said something you wish you could take back, hurt someone, killed someone, or made a bad choice because you got caught up in the passion or the lust of the moment. Maybe you just have not been nice to people. Whatever the case, if you have messed up your life, you are not alone.

Perhaps you feel that no one on earth could understand and you feel like you would rather be dead. Perhaps nothing whatsoever interests you anymore. Maybe you feel like you are on the outside of life looking in. You may feel like you are not part of life. You may feel like a zombie just going through the motions. Possibly you cry your eyes out every day, only to come back to reality and realize that you are still here and the problem has not gone away.

People who have been fortunate enough not to make bad mistakes cannot understand your feelings. Some may even have a certain prideful attitude about not having gotten into trouble. They look at you with a kind of suspicious doubt that they cannot hide.

No matter what we have done, we are still alive. We have still got to live until we die. **We cannot have any peace of mind until we overcome our defeated attitude.**

What Can We Do?

It is of the utmost importance that we take control of our lives. Many of us have given our lives over to other people, and we allow them to control us. They lay guilt on us by reminding us of our past mistakes. They put us down and we let them.

I knew a girl in prison who was a prostitute. She had a 1-year-old baby boy and she told me she wanted to turn her life around. After she left prison, I called her house one day to see how she was doing. The man who answered the phone said, "She's back out on the streets. She'll never change. She's no good and that's the way she will always be. Nobody can help her." This was the kind of encouragement the girl was getting.

My friend, you may need a dose of true encouragement. Two stories in the Bible show us how differently people can look at life and other people. In Luke, Chapter 7, a man invites Jesus to dinner. While Jesus is eating, a woman who has lived a rather loose life comes into the house and sits at the feet of Jesus. She starts crying because of her guilty feelings, and her tears wet Jesus' feet. She begins to wipe his feet with her hair and anoints them with an expensive perfume. Jesus feels compassion for her.

Meanwhile Simon, the owner of the house says to himself, "If this man were a prophet, he would know who is touching him and what kind of woman she is." Simon, like a lot of people, is self-righteous and narrowly-focused. He does everything right (in his eyes) and he cannot understand why everyone else can't be like him. He attends church regularly but he cannot see his own pride. Who would you want as your friend---Simon or Jesus?

In another revealing Bible story in John, Chapter 8, several men "catch" a woman in the act of adultery. The men take the woman to Jesus and tell him that their law says that someone caught in adultery should be stoned. Jesus says to the men, "You who have not sinned cast the first stone. Those of you who are perfect, cast the first stone. Those of you who have never messed up, throw the first stone." Slowly, all the men drop their stones and walk away because Jesus has introduced them to themselves.

What can you do if you have really messed up? **First, focus on seeing the real you again.** You probably see yourself through the eyes of other people. You may have parents who constantly call you stupid. You may have a spouse who tells you that you can't do anything right. Your friends may say, "You'll never accomplish anything." Perhaps you are the black sheep of your family, and the other members constantly put you down.

Perhaps you have heard negative comments about yourself for so long that **now you believe what others say about you is the truth**. Well, I'm here to tell you otherwise. The truth is, you are a **precious human being**.

Now, let's be honest. I know that just because I say that you are a precious person, even if I were talking to you in person right now, you would probably be skeptical. I have tried to encourage thousands of people over the years and the truth is some people change a lot and some change very little. But I invite you to consider very carefully what I am about to say to you.

If you continue being down on yourself for mistakes that you have made, people are going to run over, use, and manipulate you for as long as you feel you deserve to be treated that way. You will carry that down-trodden look and attitude, which is going to show all over your face. You will be depressed and you will cause others to feel depressed. You will make many errors in judgment. You will be more apt to abuse alcohol and drugs. You will not come anywhere near being the kind of person you could be. People will not want to be around you.

We can decide that we are *not* going to change, but we do so at a high cost. We may feel that we won't or can't change, but I am convinced that all of us have the potential to make some changes.

There are people in this life who want to love us, but we have got to give them the chance. If we push people away, we build a wall between ourselves and others. I admit it, the world is full of jerks and life is not fair. But we have still got to live here until we die.

Until you and I can see our true worth as humans, we are going to hold ourselves back from much joy, peace, and happiness. **Right this minute, if we are down on ourselves, we are holding ourselves back from living more meaningful lives.**

Making bad mistakes can give us the coldest, loneliest feelings we will ever know. Maybe you have not messed up too badly, and hopefully you won't. But if you have, I sympathize with you.

I want you to know that you can still make it. We can overcome adversity, but it's not easy. The last time I made a bad mistake, I was a "stone face" for several months. I hated life and everything about it. Sometimes I even wanted to die.

Times like these really test the stuff we are made of. **We must push on. The meaning in our lives is determined by our courage, not our mistakes. Life is not measured by our accomplishments, but by our mental toughness.**

Never give up. Adjust to your situation. The door that you closed may open up another door. **Make something else happen.**

QUESTIONS TO PONDER

- If we live our lives in self-pity, what kind of lives can we expect to have?

- If we live our lives in self-pity, what kind of lives will our children have?

- If we allow other people to hold us down because of mistakes we have made in the past, can we really expect to live a meaningful life?

- Is it possible that we are pushing people away from us and actually holding ourselves back because we are still down on ourselves because of bad choices we have made?

- Is it possible that that the bad choices we have made can lead us to make wiser choices that will bring more meaning into our lives?

- How would it help us to realize that we are human and that all of us make mistakes?

CHAPTER THIRTEEN

Just Say No!
Give Me a Break!

Alcohol and drug abuse is a major problem for many people. Many people are not able to live successfully because their lives are torn apart by addictions. It is very important that more people be aware of the difficulties that people with addictive personalities have to go through. It is also important that we do all we can to help people who suffer from problems with alcohol, drugs, and other addictions. The core problem often has a lot to do with people not feeling valued and needed.

Recently I attended a seminar for people who work in the prison ministry. During the seminar, a man read a fascinating essay on drug abuse that had been written by a high school student in Nashville, Tennessee. Everyone at the seminar thought the essay was powerful. The essay is so brutally honest and insightful that I decided to include it in this book because **I know** the essay is going to help many people. The essay also helps all of us to take a closer look at ourselves.

All of us on this planet are in this thing together. All of us need to help each other. The strong need to help the weak. Those who have a lot need to share with those who don't have much. We all need to help each other come to a deeper understanding of the meaning and purpose of life.

Life is serious business. This essay helps us see the soul and heartfelt emotions of one average individual living on this earth. I think his feelings are typical of many of us. The writer expresses some of the anguish that many people feel. He helps give us a framework from which to consider our dilemma of being human.

Read the essay slowly and thoughtfully. No matter who you are, you will probably see yourself.

Just Say No, Give Me A Break!
By Chris Mason

Drugs are a major problem among teens today, but that's nothing new. Drugs have been around and been used for ages. Our generation uses them, our parent's generation used them, some of their parents used them. Now if you compare the trends and cultures of just those three generations, drug use by teens is probably the most common factor. The question we should be asking ourselves is not, "How do we stop it?" but "Why are they doing it and how can we help that problem?" The answer is easier said than done.

First off, let's talk about what is currently being done in terms of drug prevention in teens. To be perfectly blunt, nothing. At least nothing that would remotely make a difference. Mostly because it's too late for most. I would have to say at least 75% of the teens I know smoke pot, even if it's only occasionally. Granted there are things being done in pre-teens. People tell them to "Just Say No! They tell them not to use them, they even tell them what it does to their bodies. It doesn't work. But you already know that. That's why I'm writing this paper.

All of my life, I have heard adults say, "Kids just smoke and do drugs to be cool." Well, maybe that was true for them, but not me and my friends. Mostly, we do it to forget. To forget the pain of our parent's divorce. To ease the blow of our father's fists. To deafen our ears to our mother's weeping. To make ourselves disappear and shut ourselves off from the rest of the world so we don't have to feel anymore. So we don't have to hurt anymore. Does that sound cool to you? Well, any kind of light in the darkness is cool to us. Even if we know it's the wrong one.

Adults tell us, "Don't do drugs, they will kill you. They will get you sent to jail. They will get you involved in the wrong crowd. They will ruin your memory. To most kids, this sounds like a happy invitation to a cruise vacation. It will kill us? Great. End my torment? It will get us sent to jail? Awesome. Security. It will get us involved with the wrong crowd? Wait a minute. You mean I get to be accepted as part of something? Bring it on! It will ruin your memory? Perfect. I don't want most of my memories. Don't you see, you're going about this all wrong. It can't be done from the outside in. It has to be done from the inside out.

When we were kids, we knew drugs were bad. We would never use them. Our parents were Superman and Wonder Woman. Everything was perfect. But as we got older, we started having problems. They were always there: we were just too young to know it. The problem is that we didn't have anywhere to turn to. No safe place to go and get help. So we learn to stuff it down inside and ignore it. As years go by and things get worse, we run out of room in our hearts to hide things. We still have nowhere to turn. Nowhere to offer the validation and nurturing and help we so desire. So, we turn to drugs. What else can we do? We think the drugs make these problems in our hearts disappear, when really they just put a stone wall over our hearts sealing them in.

The topic of drugs cannot be dealt with mentally at teen years. It must be dealt with emotionally early on. **Teens do drugs to get a sense of worth, to forget the pain, to bond with friends, to find a new way to enjoy life, to end life, to figure out how to answer problems, to feel loved, validated, important, special, valuable, wanted, needed, accepted, different, same, to just feel better.**

"Just say no!" What the hell does that mean? **The key is not to tell us the ways we can't escape, but to make us feel like we don't need to escape.** Lead us where to go to solve problems rather than just putting up road blocks every path we try. We become lost and helpless searching for more answers.

My solution will not be easy, but I guarantee it will be effective. Teach kids that it is okay to feel. It is okay to have emotions. Teach them the right way to handle and control these emotions. Let teachers be a safe place to go. Validate the students on an individual basis constantly. It might take time, but is it not worth it? If kids figure out early on how to communicate, deal with problems, handle stress and emotions the right way, they won't be so easily sucked toward drugs. **If they can learn early on that they all have something uniquely individual and special to offer the world, maybe they won't give up so easily.**

You might ask, "How can this be done?" I'll tell you a way that **WILL** help. Set aside class time for young children to talk about things that are bothering them or problems that they are having. Let them communicate with each other. Hearing solutions and getting support from peers is more valuable than you could imagine. Plus, it will let them know early on they are not alone. It will teach them how to communicate. It can also build lasting bonds and friends that will last for years, friends with the right foundations. The more frequently this is done, the less "stupid" it will be to them and the more it will help.

All the reasons for drug use that I have explained are the main reasons that I turned to drugs. Me! A former D.A.R.E (Drug Abuse Resistance Education) president, a leader in the F.L.A., a leader at my church, president of Power Encounter, former EXCELL member, ect. If I did it even with all of this "support," how easy would it be for someone without any support? The things I explained could help because they are things that turned me around. If I can do it, then anyone can.

I used drugs for years to dull my emotions. Now I have learned how valuable my emotions are. What I tell you will work as long as it is done the right way persistently. **School is not just preparation for college, it's preparation for life!** So, prepare them.

It all comes down to this: I am a victim of drug use. **Will you help me?**

The author of this essay reminds us that all people need to feel a sense of self-worth. People need to feel loved, important, special, wanted, needed, and accepted. People need to feel that they are unique and that they have something special to offer the world. The problem is that many people do not realize how special and unique they are.

I meet a lot of people who do not think very highly of themselves. For whatever reason, they have learned to be down on and in some cases to even hate themselves. They are losing at the game of life when all they need is a little direction and encouragement. They do not fully realize that they are going to pass this way one time, and they should make the most of their lives.

Why It Is So Difficult To Stop Taking Alcohol And Drugs

If you are truly interested in stopping alcohol or drugs, make your strongest effort to understand what I am about to say. No one wants to stop taking alcohol and drugs because they induce very pleasurable states of being.

Here is the true secret of overcoming alcohol and drugs: if we change ourselves on the inside, we will not have such a strong need to escape from life. This involves believing that we matter in life and that we are precious children of God. It involves believing that our lives have a purpose and that we are not just pathetic mistakes.

CHAPTER FOURTEEN

Aiming for Success

There is a tendency among many people today to disregard spirituality and to pursue a more pleasurable, self-seeking, self-discovery type of lifestyle. There are numerous reasons for this phenomenon--disenchantment with the way some spiritual people act, religious fanatics, scientific teaching that says the world basically created itself, teachers who claim that religion is mysticism and myth, and so on.

We have to decide for ourselves what kind of lifestyle we are going to live. It really does not matter what everyone else is doing. All of us are different. **We should seek the best reality and spirituality we can find for ourselves, our families, and our friends.**

I simply want to suggest that you consider all options in this life. Do not let the popular thinking of the time govern how you should live your life. Every choice that we make is a risk that we are taking on our own. Other people do not have all the answers. If they did, the world would not have all the problems that it does. We simply cannot live outside the laws governing the universe and relationships with people without suffering the consequences. If any of us think that we are somehow the exception to the rule, and that we can break the basic laws of life, we are going to pay a heavy price.

One of the advantages of living to be older is that we are able to look at life from different points of view. A major point I have made is that 20 or 30 years from now, most of us are not going to be anything like we are right now. I have talked to people who I had not talked to for over 20 years who have had a total change in the way they view life. Most of them usually made a change based on some traumatic event in their lives. Most became more spiritually minded and less worldly-minded.

We do not know what tomorrow may bring. I am not asking you to be spiritual. I am imploring you to consider your life, where you are in life, and how things are really going with you. Do you feel that something major may be missing?

The End Of The Matter

There is a side of life that no one can show us; we have to experience it. It comes when we shed a tear because a song is so moving. It comes when we experience the death of loved ones. We see it when we experience the true beauty of the earth and the true significance of other people rather than seeing life through the filter of our own learned feelings about the way we think things should be. In these moments, **the truth** shows itself to us. We are able to see life as it **really is.**

What is the truth? It is that all of us really do have the potential to express ourselves to the world. We may not believe it, we may deny it, we may fight it. But we do have a purpose for being here, and we do have the possibility of

contributing something to the world that no one else can.

Whether or not we overcome our shortcomings is going to determine to what degree we fulfill our purpose on earth. I am convinced that it is harder for some of us than for others. Nevertheless, all of us have to walk through life.

We truly do get to walk this earth one time. We will not pass this way again. Do not take these words lightly. I am not interested in writing eloquent words. I am interested in seeing you singing joyfully because you found out that life is about you and what you make of it.

Life is a struggle. Realize that if we are not struggling, we may not be living the best lives we can. We may not be striving to reach the level of life we are capable of reaching.

Life is not about reaching a certain point and saying, "I found it—hey, everybody, look at me."

Life is a journey of spiritual growth. Life is a journey of trying to understand ourselves. **This is not a game; our lives are at stake.** If we feel that we have already reached our destination, we are deceiving ourselves.

The world is the stage on which we play out our lives. Life comes at us from a million directions. If we are not happy, we are not against life but against ourselves.

We get one shot at life. If we aim for success we will find much of the peace and happiness that life has to offer.

Bibliography/ Suggested Reading List

Canfield, Jack. *The Success Principles*. HarperCollins Publishers, Inc., New York, NY 2005.

Lumpkin, Aaron. *Six Ways To Become All You Are Capable Of Being*. Nashville, TN, Winning Publications, 2002.

Lumpkin, Aaron. *You Can Be Positive Confident And Courageous: Learn To Lead A More Meaningful Life*. Winning Publications, Nashville, TN, 2001.

Muriel, James, Ed.D., and Jongeward, Dorothy,Ph.D. *Born To Win*. Addison-Wesley Publishing Company Inc., Phillipines 1971; Signet, New York, NY, 1978.

Norris, Chuck with Abraham, Ken. *Against All Odds*. Broadman and Holman Publishers, Nashville, TN, 2004.

Rand, Ayn. *Atlas Shrugged*. Signet, New York, NY, 1957.

The Holy Bible (King James Version).A. J. Holman Company, Philadephia, PA, 1942.

Index

S

Self-discovery: 47, 180
Self-esteem: 22, 23, 33, 109, 139
Self-worth: 22, 161, 179
Shortcomings: 8, 44, 182
Significant: 75, 147
Solomon, King: 132
Spiritual renewal: 32
Stallone, Sylvester: 132
Success: 7, 35, 64, 113, 129, 144, 148, 167

T

Tension: 64
Time: 22, 30, 31, 43, 121, 132, 134, 144
Trojan War: 91

U

Understanding: 4, 53, 106, 162

V

Vietnam War: 97

W

Waiting: 41, 55, 56
Winning: 100, 103, 106, 108
Wisdom: 4, 34, 116

About the Author

Aaron Lumpkin is a motivational, encouraging, and inspirational speaker. In addition to public speaking, he has been teaching and preaching at various state and federal prisons for almost twenty years.

Aaron's presentations motivate, encourage, and inspire people to live above- average lives. He uses straightforward, down-to-earth examples, stories and concepts. His presentations are passionate because he believes so strongly in his message.

Aaron is married to a beautiful, young lady named Judy and he has a fantastic 13-year-old son named Josh. The family resides in Nashville, Tennessee.

Aaron's main goal is to be the best motivational speaker he can be so that he can encourage people to live meaningful lives and to become the people they were meant to be.

If you would like to contact Aaron, please write or send an e-mail.

Aaron Lumpkin
P. O. Box 60443
Nashville, TN 37206-0443
Fax: 615-258-3728
E-Mail: jaaronlump@aol.com

Order Form

- Credit Card orders please call toll free: 1-800-431-1579
- Fax orders: 1-914-835-0398
- Postal Orders (checks and money orders only)
  Winning Publications
  P. O. Box 60443
  Nashville, TN 37206-0443

Please send the following: I understand that I may return any product for a full refund within 30 days.

_____ copies of *You Get One Shot At Life—Aim For Success* by Aaron Lumpkin @ $12.95 each.

_____ copies of *You Can Be Positive Confident and Courageous* by Aaron Lumpkin @ $12.95 each.

_____ copies of *Six Ways To Become All That You Are Capable of Being* CD or audio cassette tape, approximately 55 min. written and narrated by Aaron Lumpkin @ $11.95 each.

Get All Three for $26.95 for a 25% savings.

Name: _____

Address: _____

City_____ State:_____ Zip: _____

Telephone: (___)_____

Sales Tax: Tennessee residents please add 9.75%

Shipping: $3.00 for one book or tape and $2.00 for each additional item.